WHAT'S WITHIN YOU

YOUR ROADMAP TO LIVING LIFE
WITH NO BARRIERS

TOM LILLIG | DAVID SHURNA

FiNGERPRINT!

Published by
FiNGERPRINT!
An imprint of Prakash Books India Pvt. Ltd.

113/A, Darya Ganj, New Delhi-110 002,
Tel: (011) 2324 7062 – 65, Fax: (011) 2324 6975
Email: info@prakashbooks.com/sales@prakashbooks.com

facebook www.facebook.com/fingerprintpublishing
twitter www.twitter.com/FingerprintP
www.fingerprintpublishing.com

ISBN: 978 93 5440 409 2

Processed & printed in India

PRAISE FOR THE BOOK

This is an incredibly inspiring book; stories of people who refused to give up their dreams despite the daunting obstacles in their way. Each one illustrates "the indomitable human spirit," which I always cite as one of my most profound reasons for hope for humanity's future. And when you have read it, and been moved and uplifted, you will realize that you too have some of that indomitable spirit and that you too can overcome the barriers that loom ahead in your life.

—Jane Goodall, PhD, DBE, Founder of the Jane Goodall Institute, and UN Messenger of Peace

How we respond to challenges is the biggest part of life. This book coaches us to tackle our barriers head on and reminds us that what's within us is stronger than what's in our way.

—Lou Holtz, College Football Hall of Fame Coach, Speaker, Author, Analyst, and National Champion Head Coach at the University of Notre Dame

We've been fortunate to get to know the No Barriers organization and the many strong and resilient people in the community. Through its inspirational stories and how-to instruction, this book guides us on how to harness our adversity and unleash the full potential of the human spirit.

—Bob and Lee Woodruff, Peabody and Emmy-award winning ABC News Correspondent, Authors, Speakers, and Founders of the Bob Woodruff Foundation

For years, I've seen these No Barriers principles change lives—from veterans to kids to corporate leaders. If you're ready to embrace your quest for purpose no matter what is in your way, then this book is for you!

—Jamie Moldafsky,
Chief Marketing Officer of Wells Fargo Bank

No Barriers serves as a map and compass to navigate through storms and reach the summits in our lives. It's also a fast-growing movement, showing us the power of Roping Up with great people to shatter barriers and elevate the world. I know this book will help you tell your own powerful story and create a No Barriers life.

—Erik Weihenmayer, American Athlete, Adventurer,
Author, Activist, and Motivational Speaker, and the First
Unsighted Person to reach the summit of Mount Everest

This book is one of the most engaging texts I have ever read—the first pages will pull you in and ultimately empower you to change your life for the better. It is a window into the experiences, thoughts, and souls of people who will profoundly inspire you. It speaks to your brain and your heart. It is a magical gift of fuel and direction for life—not a "how-to" book. Read it at your peril—your life will likely not be the same when you are done.

—George Heinrichs, CEO of ANDE,
and Founder of Intrado, Inc.

This book is a brave and bold statement from some of the most incredible people you will ever read about. Their stories of life, adventure, and triumph over adversity will touch your heart and inspire you to look at the world in a different way.

—Casey Harris,
Unsighted Keyboardist for X Ambassadors

The great Sir Winston Churchill once remarked that courage is the first of human qualities, for it is the one that ensures all the rest. In this book, you will read of true courage embodied in the No Barriers philosophy—the courage to face down adversity, the courage to overcome one's doubts and fears, and the courage to do what others tell you cannot be done. Here you will find inspiration and lessons for a lifetime.

—Dr. Donald Morel, Chairman and CEO (retired)
West Pharmaceutical Services Inc.

No Barriers is an embodiment of inspiration, hope, and perseverance. This book shares in-depth how everyone can recognize the power they have to make a positive impact on the world, no matter who you are or what challenges you may face, and that's what I love the most about the No Barriers message.

—Maya Penn, Oprah Supersoul 100 Entrepreneur,
and CEO of Maya's Ideas

This book teaches us to look deep within ourselves to find our strength, resilience, and purpose. It shows us how to turn our big challenges into our biggest triumphs. Being a part of No Barriers has changed my life, and I know people will be positively impacted by this book.

—Mandy Harvey, award-winning Deaf Singer, Songwriter, and Motivational Speaker, and *America's Got Talent* Performer with over 500 million views

What's Within You is a must-read for anyone wanting to lead a purposeful, integrated life. The stories are compelling and serve to highlight the timeless, practical, and life-changing No Barriers concepts.

—Greg Brenneman, Board Chair of Home Depot, and Former Chairman, CEO, President and/or COO of Quiznos Sub, Burger King, PwC Consulting, and Continental Airlines, and Executive Chairman of CCMP Capital

This book captures the spirit of hope, possibility, and courage that I feel we should all live by. It's both inspirational and practical, providing powerful tools to help each of us break through the barriers we face. Love it.

—Luis Gallardo, Former Global CMO for Deloitte, and Founder of the World Happiness Fest

The people profiled in this book are the ultimate barrier busters—they inspire each of us to strive to be the best version of ourselves. The principles and tools provided will empower you to break through your adversities and tap into your full potential.

—Dr. Paul Stoltz, Author of five international bestselling books on grit and resilience, and Founder of Peak Learning

No Barriers challenges us to believe in a future that does not yet exist. And this book gives us the confidence to know we can get there.

—Dr. Hugh Herr, *Time* magazine's Leader of the Bionic Age, MIT Professor, and Founder of BionX

I have always loved the No Barriers' message and have been fortunate to attend many of their events. I know their programs transform lives for the better, and this book delivers just as powerfully. Now more than ever, we need books like this one to remind us that even in the face of tremendous obstacles, we must harness our challenges and unleash the power of the human spirit to unlock our infinite self.

—Kyle Maynard, two-time *ESPY* Award-Winner, and Author of the *New York Times* bestseller, *No Excuses*

My work with No Barriers consistently reminds me that our greatest struggles may, in fact, be our greatest strengths— and give us the ability to create meaningful change in ourselves and the world. This book is a true testament that no matter how dark it may seem, the light of the human spirit conquers all.

—Katie Hnida, Author, Speaker, and the First Woman to play and score points in an NCAA football game

There are a few moments in my life I will never forget, and my first introduction to No Barriers is definitely one of them. I was at my first No Barrier Summit. I was surrounded by people who were blind, deaf, missing limbs—every sort of classic "disability" you could imagine. Now imagine getting my ass and ego handed to me throughout the weekend while these same people outdid me in every competition and challenge we were presented. I quickly learned—and will never forget—that "what is within you is stronger than what is in your way." I preach and believe that nothing is impossible. The people of No Barriers and the lessons of this book demonstrate what it means to truly overcome your own impossible, and live a life with No Barriers.

—Mick Ebeling, Founder of Not Impossible Labs

This book shows you how to find your passion and purpose and dream the impossible. The No Barrier spirit will remind you that you can't ever fail if you never stop trying.

—Rich Goodstone, Co-Founder of Superfly Productions and the Bonnaroo Music & Arts Festival

The philosophy of No Barriers is interchangeable with the principles of what it means to be a TeamUSA athlete. I know the stuff in this book works because it unlocked an inferno inside me I never knew existed, and made me into a Paralympian! The single greatest regret I have in life is that I didn't find the No Barriers mindset sooner.

—Bill Lister III, Paralympic Road and Track Cyclist

We must always set goals and dedicate ourselves fully to achieving them. Tom and David remind us in this book that even when we get knocked down, we must bounce back up, ready to tackle our next challenge.

—Rudy Ruettiger, the inspiration behind the movie Rudy

Gains are hard. We know this. From our relationships with our friends, co-workers, and ourselves, to the gym and how we interact with the ever-changing world, there are many obstacles that slow our growth. What's Within You offers nerve and soul-stirring tales of perseverance and achievement through myriad challenges, inspiring hope, and becoming a springboard to leading a more purposeful and fulfilled journey.

—Mike Harmon, Host with FOX Sports Radio,
and Creator of FindYourWins.com

The vision to see obstacles as opportunities doesn't come easily. It's hard to see how our challenges can have positive impacts, especially when we are staring at them seemingly alone. It is why the No Barriers community has become a part of my life. If you are looking for a virtual rope team to help you navigate through life's challenges, this book is for you.

—Heather Thomson, Entrepreneur, Health and Wellness
Coach, Reality Star, Adventurer, and Philanthropist

As a retired superintendent and high school principal, I read What's Within You from the perspective of a school leader and realized what a great resource the book would be for school superintendents, principals, and department chairs as they set their vision as educational leaders in the ever-evolving school improvement process. I would recommend What's Within You as a primer for school leaders to develop their mission statement and use the seven life elements as a roadmap to develop a vision for a school district, school, or academic department and also as a way to assess the success of the vision. I especially found valuable the concept of Summit, the life element that suggests looking backward to celebrate the success that a person or institution has achieved. Too frequently in education, we plow forward without celebrating the successes of our efforts.

—Thomas R. Dixey,
Retired Chicago School Superintendent

For Tina Lillig

and

Every reader who does not yet believe

What's Within You Is Stronger Than
What's In Your Way

One hundred per cent of the proceeds of this book support
No Barriers, a nonprofit organization.

Contents

Contents

Acknowledgments

This is a book that couldn't exist without the No Barriers organization. We want to thank the No Barriers staff, board, participants, donors, and volunteers who make our mission possible. Throughout the book writing process, we felt like we were channelling the energy of the organization as much as we were putting down our own ideas. In truth, the No Barriers philosophy is the result of tens of thousands of people who have made the organization a part of their lives.

So, we'd like to start by thanking our participants and their families for trusting us to deliver life-changing programs to you. Many of you came to us at a vulnerable time in your lives, and we are honoured that you believed enough in No Barriers to give our programs a shot. We have learned so much from you in this journey. You are truly No Barriers.

A special thanks to our No Barriers participants and ambassadors who are featured in these pages. They opened up their stories to us, and we have been changed forever as a result.

No Barriers is built on the shoulders of the giants who started this movement back in 2003 including, though not limited to, Jim Goldsmith, Mark Wellman, Wayne Hanson, Paolo Pompanin, Ugo Pompanin, Miki Maioni, Alessandra Urbancich, Maruo di Baisi, and Hugh Herr.

Erik Weihenmayer has done more than any other individual to help us build No Barriers. Most importantly for this book, he has been the primary driver and creator of the principles that we teach. With him by our side, we've honed and tweaked the way we all learn and apply the No Barriers Life to our own lives. And we've grown the movement exponentially due to many of the connections Erik masterfully makes. Thanks to Erik's team at Touch the Top, especially Ellie Weihenmayer, Ed Weihenmayer, Skyler Williams, and Pauline Shaffer who work closely with No Barriers every week. They are constantly testing and tweaking our principles so that we make them as relevant and powerful as possible.

Thanks to Sasha Rabchevksy for being a tireless voice for accessibility and to Bill Barkeley for the adventures you inspired over many years of board service.

Thanks to Julie Dubin. Without Julie, we may never have been involved in this work. Dave first met Julie through their graduate studies at Duke, and it was her vision and commitment to quality that built the foundation of this organization. Most importantly, she ensured that every program we ever deliver would truly change lives.

Thanks to our many donors and sponsors who have helped shape this movement over the years. Your financial support makes No Barriers programs possible. If you've ever contributed to our movement, whether $1 or $1,000,000, we are grateful for your commitment. And thanks to our fearless development team led by Cindy Bean for all their work building and growing our supporter base.

Over the years, the No Barriers staff have helped us put our principles into the field forcing us to test and measure their success. It is always an iterative process, and we will forever be thankful for the full-time staff, board, expedition leaders, and volunteers who bring the curriculum to life in our programs. A very special thanks to Andrea Delorey who has spent more time than perhaps any other human being thinking about how to apply the No Barriers Life principles to all the populations that we serve.

We are grateful to Dr. Mat Duerden and Dr. Neil Lundberg from Brigham Young University for working with us for nearly ten years to study the short- and long-term impact of our No Barriers philosophy on our programs. Their research continues to hone our principles and makes our programs better and better.

A special thanks to Chris Frazier who embodies the No Barriers motto and helped us take our ideas and formulate them into an actual book. If anyone ever needs help on a manuscript, he should be your man. Beyond being an awesome writer, he is thoughtful, meticulous, and creative. And he just gets it done!

Thanks to the members of the Club de Tobi for reminding us to follow our dreams and that all is well. The laughter, tears, and adventures we share are hidden in these pages.

I (Dave) would like to thank my wife Gina for showing me a pathway through the darkest of times, for raising an incredible family, and for affording me the space and time to build No Barriers. To James and Clara for reminding me to be a kid again and for the love, gratitude, and affection they share with me every day. To my mom and dad for teaching me what it means to live a life dedicated to serving others. To my brother for making me laugh. To Meg, Stan, and Jen for hitchhiking across Africa with me and giving me the space to craft my life vision while in Malawi—this book completes that circle. And to Flash for bringing me to Colorado. To Uncle Lou for reminding me to follow my dreams. To Uncle Ken for teaching me the value of attending to people's suffering. Thanks to Howard Drossman and Julie Francis for trusting me to build the Catamount Institute and to Michael Hannigan, Howard, and Julie for everything I learned about building a nonprofit organization as a result. Thanks finally to Tom Lillig for the many hours of work he has put into No Barriers over the years including branding workshops, strategic planning, emergency planning, and so much more. This book was Tom's idea and his gift to the organization, and we will forever be grateful for everything he has contributed.

I (Tom) would like to thank my wife Cindy for being an amazingly selfless, strong, and supportive partner and for the overflowing love she has for our family. To Coleman, Valentino, and Matia—I hold each of your beautiful spirits so close to my heart, and I thank you for giving me such great joy every time we play. To my mom for teaching me to fall in love with your calling, and to my dad for being the ultimate example of how to be a person for others. To my brothers and their families for binding all of us together through the ups and the downs with love, laughter, gentleness, and oatmeal cake. To Joel Humowiecki for always being clutch, though I was safe at home. To Sharif Nijim for teaching me that great friends can become *fratelli*. To Debra Bork for your willingness to fight for me when I couldn't speak. To Larry Stone and Millie Ward for showing me how to be a leader who serves. To Kyle Floyd for being the visionary designer behind the No Barriers brand. To Jim Connelly for teaching me everything I know about dedication and perseverance. Thanks to my teachers from Alcuin Montessori, Emerson, St. Ignatius College Prep, and the University of Notre Dame. Finally, to Dave for inviting me to be his No Barriers co-pilot for almost two decades, the most LORE-filled adventure of my life.

Thanks to the wonderful folks on the Scribe team including Rikki, Kayla, and Tucker who jump-started the publishing process for us and gave us a swift kick in the butt to get this finished and in the hands of readers who need it.

The *What's Within You* Manifesto

When the cruel winds of life knock us down,
When harsh words or harsher indifference
make us feel small,
When fear of the unknown paralyzes our spirit,
And when the shame of our scars crushes all hope,
In these moments of darkness, we courageously look
inside ourselves to find a hidden light.
That light reveals a will to live, a love of self, a desire to
grow, and a willingness to try.
We choose to embrace our struggle wholeheartedly,
and with shattered bones and hurt feelings,
we continue moving forward.
For it is our suffering that makes us stronger, and our
many falls that fuel our rise.
We draft ourselves into service, passionate warriors for
our communal potential.
We come together under our proud but tattered flag,
bound by both our brokenness and our bravery.
Marching toward the challenge and guided by our light,
we are fearless, resilient, and unstoppable, because
**What's Within Us Is Stronger
Than What's In Our Way.**

Introduction

What's Within You

119104—this was the prisoner identification number assigned to Viktor Frankl when he was arrested and transported to a Nazi concentration camp in 1942. Along with his wife and his parents, Frankl was taken from his home in Vienna and forced to live through what he called the "misery of our time." Over the course of the next three years, Frankl observed the mental and physical effects of the dehumanizing treatment that he and other prisoners had to endure in the camps. And what he concluded was this: those prisoners who maintained a rich inner life and a sense of purpose from day to day were more likely to survive, whereas those who lost faith in the future and therefore lost meaning in their lives perished.

For Frankl, purpose gave prisoners an armour to defend against the onslaught of unthinkable challenges in the concentration camps. With so little value put on them by the Nazis, it was imperative that the prisoners placed an even greater personal value on their own lives. The prisoners had to find that spark within them—their reason for living—no matter how all-consuming the darkness became. And if against all odds they could keep that spark lit, then they were better equipped to overcome the near-impossible adversity they faced. As Nietzsche once mused, "He who has a *why* to live for can bear almost any *how*."

After World War II, Viktor Frankl counted himself as one of the lucky few who survived the Holocaust. He lost his pregnant wife, his parents, and his brother to the Nazis, along with the nearly six million other Jews who were killed. Upon his return to Vienna, Frankl—who already had a background in neurology and psychiatry before the war—set out to capture his experience and the experiences of many other prisoners in his seminal work, *Man's Search for Meaning*. And in his exploration of the subject, he struck upon a common refrain: the ability to overcome challenges is directly related to a person's ability to find meaning within themselves.

Frankl's insights seem more relevant today than ever before. The COVID-19 pandemic has threatened the lives and the livelihoods of people around the globe in new and profound ways. In addition to the obvious damage that the virus has had on the physical health of patients, it also has compromised the emotional and mental well-being of millions more around the world. Feelings of fear, helplessness, and grief have spread from country to country, further upending people's lives. In a poll taken just weeks after the outbreak, nearly half of all adults in the United States reported that their mental health had been negatively impacted due to worry and stress.

While Frankl's circumstance was obviously very different than that of a health pandemic, he understood that regardless of the situation, there was a "human capacity to creatively turn life's negative aspects into something positive or constructive." In short, he knew that the secret to getting through suffering was not to escape it or run away from it but rather to turn into it and find positive meaning in it. For some, that could be an opportunity to reflect and recalibrate one's priorities, foster a deeper connection to our loved ones, or let go of some unhealthy habits that we have been carrying. Frankl reminds us that in the face of challenges that seem insurmountable, we have an opportunity to choose our response, and our choice should reflect our purpose.

So, Frankl's legacy is found in the irreplaceable significance of purpose and its inherent connection to how humans break through adversity. And in the years since the publication of Frankl's revelatory book, his ideas have been (wittingly or unwittingly) appropriated by people and companies worldwide. Everyone from sports psychologists to advertisers to personal growth gurus and influencers have tapped into Frankl's concepts of purpose and adversity. But more often than not, they only scratch the surface of the subject, and they fail to answer the hard questions:

How do you discover your purpose? Once you have found your purpose, how do you use it as a catalyst for real, measurable change in your life—to activate the best version of yourself? Or to help you effectively confront your toughest challenges? And, also: How do you find the right community to help support you in your newfound purpose?

Almost twenty years ago, we helped cofound a nonprofit organization that would answer these very questions. The organization, which would eventually become known as No Barriers, set out to create transformative experiences for people in search of direction and purpose and in doing so, assist them in overcoming the adversity they were confronting in their lives.

In the early days of the organization, we worked most often with wounded veterans as well as youth across all backgrounds. We ran programs geared toward improving the lives of veterans with disabilities, providing experiences in challenging environments that pushed them to explore their own sense of purpose, and helped them tackle personal tribulations. And we led curriculum-based adventures for teens and young adults—some struggling with social challenges, others with economic barriers—helping them to develop the tools necessary to transition into adulthood and the larger world around them.

But over the years, we began to realize that the positive impact our programs were having on the lives of our participants could be valuable beyond the spheres of veterans and students. And so, we expanded our mission and opened up the No Barriers tent to all those in search of ways to overcome adversity.

Today, we work with tens of thousands of people each year, guiding them through our seven Life Elements as they learn the built-in connection between living a purpose-driven life and our ability to break through barriers. Recently, we have noticed an uptick in the numbers of people who are seeking out our organization and what we do.

It could be that many of us are searching everywhere but within ourselves for meaning: our phones, our diets, the shows we watch, social media, or the celebrities or gurus we follow. And none of it provides a lasting sense of meaning. All those things will get you to Wednesday, but then you'll be hungry for more. As E.O. Wilson has said, we're all drowning in information while starving for wisdom.

But here's the other thing. While there is seemingly no end to the amount of books and blogs out there that promise a better you or offer quick-and-easy life makeovers, they often fall short in addressing the full picture. You can find books about purpose, meaning, and happiness, and you can find books about how to break through some current adversity you're facing (addiction, marital problems, financial challenges, etc.). But what's missing is a book that gives us a map to navigate the gap between our idealistic aspirations for a life of purpose and the realistic barriers that get in our way.

Ultimately, what we realized—and what pushed us to write this book—is that there are no books out there that achieve the success of our program's empirical, hands-on approach that has helped so many people reorient their lives toward a larger purpose.

Over the years, we have worked closely with researchers to help evaluate the impact of our program on our participants. This has provided us with reams of data proving the power of all aspects of our model, and we will be sharing that research throughout each chapter.

But for now, at the start of your journey with this book, here are two data points that showcase the general impact of No Barriers's philosophies and methods:

1. A solid ninety-five per cent of our participants say that our programs changed their lives forever. From the business executives who discover a new way to lead with purpose through adversity, to veterans who describe the way our program literally saved them from suicide, these principles are powerful and universal. And they matter. If you take the time to apply the ideas and lessons in this book to your life, you too will be changed forever.

2. An overwhelming majority of our participants (ninety per cent) leave our programs agreeing or strongly agreeing with the idea that "what's within me is stronger than what's in my way." Forty-five per cent more participants believe in this after their No Barriers experience than before. This is even more remarkable when you

consider that the majority of our participants are facing tremendous challenges in their lives—from terminal illnesses to disabilities, substance abuse to poverty. Imagine discovering your own ability to tap into a mindset that knows that no matter the adversity you might face, you're stronger than it. That's the power of the principles herein.

For us, *What's Within You* fills the needs of our current moment. And as you read this book, you can be confident that our concepts rely on profound practice and feedback.

WHO SHOULD READ THIS BOOK?

The short answer: *all of us*. We all face challenges in our lives, whether great or small. None of us is immune to struggle. Adversity doesn't care about race, class, creed, or gender. It doesn't care about where you come from, what your job title is, what abilities or resources you may have. This is a simple fact of life: if you walk this planet, you face challenges on a daily basis.

The next time you're riding a crowded bus, or waiting in line at the coffee shop, or sitting in the stands at a football game, look right and look left, and you will see people struggling—whether internally or externally—with all kinds of issues in their lives. The person to your right might be struggling in their marriage or dealing with a difficult co-worker. Perhaps that person is wrestling with body image issues or battling an addiction to alcohol. The person to your left might be weathering the recent loss of a parent or child or coping with the stress of being unable to make rent that month. Or perhaps that person has just returned from serving abroad in the military and now he or she is struggling to assimilate back into normal everyday life in a way that makes them feel whole and needed.

Maybe these people are struggling with issues just like yours, or maybe they're struggling with issues you've never had to face. Either way, all of us need the tools to overcome these challenges. And as hard as this is to believe, most of us are never taught what the tools are, nor are we equipped to use these tools. In the pages ahead, you will find tried-and-tested methods and strategies designed specifically to help you push through any obstacle you suddenly find in your way.

The other reason this book applies to people of all stripes: *every one of us needs purpose*. It's another one of those enduring facts of life, and there's just no getting around it. Although some of us may try to live on bread and water alone (or perhaps a diet of social media *likes*), such an approach to life does not provide the sustenance we truly need to survive. Without a sense of purpose, we often feel like we are wandering the forest without a compass; or worse, we feel stuck—we find ourselves paralyzed by an unfillable emptiness that prevents us from taking action at all.

Recent research has shown that having purpose and meaning in life increases your emotional well-being and overall life satisfaction. Having meaning in your life improves your mental and physical health, enhances your resilience and self-esteem, and decreases your chances of suffering from depression. And in our many years of working with people to help them fight through challenges, we have learned that a sense of purpose has been the key ingredient in breaking through their barriers.

So, in this book, we have two overarching goals:

- First, we will help you to access that thing inside you that provides meaning for you. Since purpose is not a one-size-fits-all proposition, this will be a discovery process specific to your life and to your personal needs. We will guide you through a process of deep internal considerations and practical exercises that will reflect your views and values back to you, and you will then use your own set of values to reveal that thing inside of you that will become your guiding star. Whether you know it or not, you already have the raw materials of meaning and purpose within you; sometimes it's hiding there in the dark, and you just need a flashlight to help you find it. We will be that flashlight.

- Second, we will show you how to use that sense of purpose as a strategy for overcoming any challenge that life might send your way. In doing so, we will help you become the best version of yourself, one that is forged through the crucible of adversity. Because here's what we know, and what brain research and personal performance studies support: stress and adversity help you grow developmentally. In the words of Albert Einstein, "Adversity introduces a man to himself." It's how you respond to adversity, how you embrace it, and how you manage it that reveals your character and determines if it strengthens you or sidelines you in life. Your full potential is waiting just on the other side of all those seemingly impenetrable barriers. We will give you the tools that help you break through those barriers.

To boil it down, this is a book for people who: (a) *have committed to live a full and meaningful life but are struggling because some barrier has derailed them;* or (b) *have a gut feeling that there's a way to live differently—to live a life full of purpose—but they can't quite put their finger on how to do it.*

This is a book about the interplay between purpose and persistence and how managing to balance these two dichotomies unleashes our fullest potential.

THE LIFE ELEMENTS

So, for nearly two decades now, we have been working with people in search of ways to overcome adversity in their lives and discover meaning within themselves. In that time, our objective within the organization has remained constant. The questions that first started us on this journey have not changed. But the answers have evolved naturally through trial and error and through our interactions and experiences within the No Barriers community.

In a sense, the organization became a rigorous test kitchen, where we would see in real time what ingredients worked best to help people overcome challenges. Almost twenty thousand people have passed through the doors of that kitchen. Year over year, we sat with participants and engaged with their struggles. We listened to them in their lowest moments, when they felt the most lost or overwhelmed by obstacles, and we worked with them to refine strategies and tools that wouldn't just get them through that moment but also get them through the rest of their journey.

And the result is a recipe that we call the seven *Life Elements*:

VISION. In discovering your purpose, you need to learn the difference between what you want to *do* in life and what you want to *be*. Most of us have been oriented toward living life through a collection of goals: some tasks get us through the day; a checklist might get us through the week; and New Year's resolutions will get us through, well . . . January. But what happens after that? What allows you to keep focused month after month and year after year? *Vision* is about allowing your core values to reveal a foundational and sustainable purpose for your life.

REACH. Once you have cracked the code on purpose, how do you use that new understanding of yourself to confront your challenges? How do you step outside of your comfort zone and fully acknowledge the obstacles that have been keeping you from your best self? With *Reach*, you will grab hold of the adversity that is in your life right now; and, in doing so, you will prepare yourself to overcome those challenges.

ALCHEMY. By this point, you have discovered your purpose, you have confronted your problems head-on. Now it's time to make sure you have developed the right mindset to move forward. If a skillset is the thing you can see and do, mindset is why and how you do what you do, and that is what you will focus on in this element. In ancient times, alchemy was the process of transforming base metals into gold. For us, *Alchemy* is about the ability to have hope and optimism in the face of adversity.

PIONEERING. In the best of possible worlds, once you are able to acknowledge the problems in your life, a solution would simply present itself to you, much like an elementary mathematical equation. It can be that easy, right? *If only*. Instead, life asks you to invent unique solutions that fit your purpose. *Pioneering* is about developing systems, strategies, and tools that will help you find creative ways to work through even your toughest challenges.

ROPE TEAM. Few things in life are as difficult as admitting that you need the support of others. You like to think that you can do it all on your own, and you might even believe that asking for help is a form of weakness. We are here to tell you that seeking out support is actually a strength. Creating a supportive network around you takes real courage as you entrust others with your Vision. As you develop your *Rope Team*, you will discover how to be the best version of yourself in the company of those who support you.

SUMMITS. Oftentimes when you are on your journey, you are so focused on the road ahead that you forget to stop every once in a while and look back at how you got here. *Summits* is about reflecting on your journey even when you may still be in the middle of it, because sometimes in those moments of reflection, you will recognize Summits that you didn't realize you had passed along the way.

ELEVATE. Until now, this journey has been about looking inward and helping you grow toward a better version of yourself. But there comes a point where it's time to lift others up as well. There is an energy in helping others: by giving of yourself, you are gaining a fuller sense of who you truly are. This is the moment where your perspective turns from focusing inward to focusing outward. *Elevate* is about taking what you have learned on your journey and sharing it with those around you. Just as others have supported you along the way, now it is time for you to become a part of someone else's support system.

Each of these *Life Elements* holds a unique significance in your efforts to overcome adversity. Taken individually, they can certainly benefit your life in meaningful ways. Having *Vision* will provide you with a sense of direction, to find that compass we so desperately need. *Pioneering* will help you understand how to create solutions to complex problems. *Elevate* will open your eyes to the wider community around you. But for optimal results— to truly experience the journey offered in the pages ahead—you will want to complete all seven of the *Life Elements*. As Aristotle tells us, the whole is greater than the sum of its parts. And it is only the full combination of these *Life Elements* that will produce the total and desired effect.

WHAT TO EXPECT

In the chapters ahead, we will explore the Life Elements through many different lenses. At the start of each chapter, we will introduce you to people who we believe exemplify the spirit of one of the elements. You will discover the story of a biophysicist who—driven by the loss of his legs—invented the most technologically advanced prosthetics to date so that he could climb again; or the inspirational account of a wounded veteran who was burned over the majority of his body, yet still found a way to transform his outlook from one of suffering to one of joy as he found a career in entertainment. You will read about an aspiring music teacher who lost her hearing in college but went on to experience global success as a singer-songwriter; or a plus-size actress who worked hard to overcome her own body image issues in order to promote positivity and empowerment for others through dancing and her own television show. And in a story that defies believability, you will learn about a blind man who followed his passion to climb the tallest mountains in the world and kayak the most challenging rapids.

But while we want to show you the extraordinary success stories, we also want to show you the ordinary ones, too; because sometimes, hearing those stories can be equally if not more instructive in how you face challenges on a daily basis. These are the everyday heroes who have come to the No Barriers community with stories of addiction, or loss, or career burnout, and then managed to reorient their lives in ways they never thought possible. Over the course of the book, we want to track the progress of others who have gone through the same journey you are about to take.

In addition to the uplifting profiles and case studies, we will explore some of the scientific and philosophical foundations of the Life Elements. While this is by no means an academic book, much of our concepts have been founded on considerable empirical evidence, and we have been working with external researchers to study the short- and long-term impact of our model over the course of ten years. In each chapter, these data points will help underscore why each Life Element matters.

We also want to include classical foundations and the age-old wisdom that helped to inform the Life Elements as we developed them. Therefore, this section will include teachings from people we are designating as our *Grand*

Philosophers. You can take comfort in knowing that the structural bones of our concepts originate in fundamental principles that have been explored for thousands of years. The problems we are helping you solve in this book are timeless struggles with which some of history's greatest philosophers, scientists, and leading religious figures have wrestled; and the good news is that there are universal truths—supported by both modern-day research and ancient wisdom—on which you can rely.

And finally, we will end each chapter with practical exercises and prompts that will help you achieve each of the Life Elements. Because, first and foremost, this book is prescriptive. We will lead you through activities and questions that will help you reshape your understanding of who you are and what drives you in life.

WHAT'S IN YOUR WAY?

Now comes the hard part. As the Greeks say, you must suffer your way to freedom. In the pages ahead, we will ask a lot of you. If at any point you find yourself saying, "Wow, this seems easy," then you're not doing it right. Finding your purpose is one of life's greatest challenges. Being completely honest with yourself can often be emotionally taxing. But we promise, this book is as rewarding as it is tough. In success, this will become a dog-eared handbook you find yourself coming back to over and over again as life presents you with setbacks and unexpected obstacles that we all must face.

And ultimately, like the thousands of participants we serve every year, as you read this book, you'll come to discover this guiding principle:

What's Within You Is Stronger Than
What's In Your Way.

CHAPTER ONE

Vision

"The most pathetic person in the world is someone
who has sight but no vision."
—*Helen Keller*

BELIEVING IS SEEING

"I can't see."

It was the week before Erik Weihenmayer's
freshman year of high school, and he had woken
up one morning to discover that he had lost his
sight completely. Even though he could feel the
sun on his face, and the curtains were open for
the dawn to greet him, everything was black—
not even a hint of morning light. He called
out to his parents, and when they entered, he

revealed the news to them: he was finally, and officially, blind.

The truth was, Erik, a floppy-haired teenager, had been going blind since he was a young child. At three years old, the doctors had diagnosed him with retinoschisis, a rare congenital eye disease that would cause his retinas to slowly detach at the centre of his pupils. Low-vision specialists had predicted that he would lose the last of his sight sometime in his early teens. Even though Erik had willed himself to believe that he could beat the prognosis, that time was now.

In that moment, when the last bit of Erik's vision had finally abandoned him, he was consumed by two very distinct emotions, each battling it out for supremacy. The first emotion was relief. He had been living somewhere between blindness and sight for most of his life, and for much of that time, he lived in fear of the day his sight would be gone completely. Well, that day had now come, so there was no use fearing it anymore; hence, *relief.*

However, Erik was also angry. He resented the fact that he could no longer see, while those around him could. When he was led into school on his first day of freshman year, he could hear all the sounds of laughter, excitement, and adventure bouncing around the halls; and for him, he was just hearing all the things he was going to miss out on now. Erik felt like he had been condemned to a dark prison, sentenced to listen to others live their lives as he missed out on his own.

So, while relief and anger both tugged on Erik in those early days of blindness, it was his anger that won out—at least initially. This anger led to denial.

Like most of us, Erik didn't want to admit to his adversity. For a while, it was easier that way. At home and at school, he refused to acknowledge the new reality of his life. When his parents encouraged him to use a cane, he did so begrudgingly; and often, he would intentionally break his cane or throw it away, forcing his parents to continually get new ones. He was also reluctant to learn braille. And at school, he eschewed help from teachers and other students. In his mind, their words had a veneer of pity, and if he accepted their assistance, he would be admitting he was pitiable.

But denying his adversity was a short-term, ineffective solution—lesson he would learn the hard way, and more than once. Erik describes one such incident: he was playing out on a dock with friends, refusing to use his cane, when he suddenly fell off the dock, flipped over in the air, and landed hard on the deck of a boat. Another time, Erik was trying to navigate the hallways at school in search of a bathroom. But because he stubbornly turned down help from classmates and teachers, Erik didn't make it to the bathroom in time, and he wet himself. Erik's denial was only leading him to greater pain and embarrassment, but still, he insisted on lying to himself.

Then, finally, the truth hit him in the face. Literally.

One day, Erik was riding home from school in a van designated for disabled students by the district. As was his habit at the time, Erik was complaining to the driver. Erik told the driver he wasn't blind and that he belonged on a bus with his sighted friends. The driver, having grown tired of Erik's constant haranguing, pulled off to the side of the road and had Erik step from the van. Suddenly, Erik felt a basketball bounce off his face. The driver stated the obvious, "Erik, you can't catch a basketball. You're blind." The words were harsh, but they were true. Then the driver instructed Erik to hold out his hands, preparing him to catch the ball. He threw the basketball, and Erik caught it in his readied hands. The driver said, "Erik, stop fighting people. Let people help you." Thanks to his driver's brutal honesty, Erik finally saw the reality of his situation cast into high relief—denying his disability was stifling any chance of him succeeding in life. To transcend his adversity, he first had to embrace it.

From that day forward, Erik wanted to define himself by what he *could* do, not by what he *couldn't*. As he says in his memoir, *Touch the Top of the World*, "The things I could not do, I would let go; but the things I could do, I would learn to do well." And it was this shift in mindset that prompted Erik to try out for the wrestling team.

For the longest time, doctors had cautioned Erik against participating in contact sports because of the potential for further damage to his retinas. But now that Erik had lost his sight completely, there was no more risk to his eyes. While basketball and football were out for obvious reasons, wrestling was a sport for which Erik was well suited. In fact, it played to his strengths. It was a sport where feeling and touch mattered more than sight. In addition, hearing could be an asset. Erik could locate his opponent by the sound of their footfalls on the mat.

With the encouragement of his parents, Erik joined the wrestling team. To the shock of his classmates, Erik would ultimately prove to be a skilled and competitive wrestler. While the 142-pound Erik went 0–15 in his first year on the team, he continued to train and improve. By his senior year, Erik would notch thirty-three pins and be named team captain. He even went on to compete in the National Junior Freestyle Wrestling Championships.

But nearly two years after Erik lost his vision, he would have to endure an even greater tragedy. While Erik was away at wrestling camp one summer, he received an urgent call from his father: his mother had been in a car accident and she didn't survive. Erik was devastated. It was like a bad dream for him. He had just regained a sense of who he could be after going blind—in no small part because of his mother—and now he was adrift again. For Erik, his mother played a unique role in his life. Where his father was the broom pushing Erik to go beyond his limits, his mother was the dustpan, always there to pick him up if he failed. As he says, "If I had gone blind a thousand times, the pain would have been nothing in comparison." His mother had been a guiding light for him and an irreplaceable source of strength. Now that his mother was gone, he would have to heal all over again. It wasn't fair.

A short time after his mother passed, Erik received a newsletter from an organization that was offering to take blind teens rock climbing. His first thought was, "Who would be crazy enough to take a blind kid rock climbing?" His second thought was, "Why not?" So, he signed himself up.

To Erik's surprise, he took to the rock like a duck to water. As his hands passed over the grooves and edges of the rock face in search of holds, he realized that climbing was not so different from reading braille. Just like the raised dots he had learned to interpret, the indentations and bumps in the rocks held information for him. With climbing, Erik's hands officially became his eyes, and it felt empowering. He was able to see the wall in ways that sighted people might not. And from wrestling, he was lean and agile with natural upper body strength, which also gave him an edge on the rock. And on top of the physical challenge, Erik enjoyed solving the puzzle of the rock, his hands piecing together the wider picture of the wall.

So, Erik began climbing at the age of sixteen. And from then on, he was hooked.

After high school, Erik would go off to college in Boston. Over the next few years, he continued to climb, pulling his way up to new heights. On his summer breaks, he would travel with his father and brothers to far-off places and they would climb together. One such climb was in Peru, where they did three mountain passes in five days. Next, it was on to the Baltoro Glacier in Pakistan. And then, the Highlands of Irian Jaya.

By the time he graduated college and moved to Arizona for a teaching job at a high school in the suburbs of Phoenix, Erik began setting his sights on some of the more challenging climbs around the globe. He trained in Arizona, Colorado, and Utah, hoping that he could build up the stamina and strength to climb the tallest mountain in North America—Denali, which stands proud at over 20,000 feet in the Alaska Range. After a month-long gruelling training regimen, Erik and a climbing team started their ascent of Denali. Nineteen days later, Erik reached the summit of that mountain, on a day that turned out to be Helen Keller's birthday. That successful climb gave Erik the confidence to continue his attempts to climb the Seven Summits, the tallest mountains on each continent. He would soon conquer Aconcagua in South America as well as Kilimanjaro in Africa. (Side note: Erik has a bit of a romantic streak in him, and he married his now-wife, Ellie, some 13,000 feet in the air while climbing Kilimanjaro.) With these famed mountaintops under his boots, Erik had become a *bona fide* mountaineer; blind or not, he was starting to feel unstoppable.

And then came Everest.

For most of us, Mount Everest is just a metaphor, typically reserved for the greater challenges we might face in our lives. For Erik, it was 29,000 feet of rock, snow, and ice rising out of the Himalayas that he had dreamed of climbing since his earliest days of mountaineering. But that dream felt so remote, so impossible that he didn't even dare utter the words aloud—not even to his wife, Ellie.

Erik knew that climbing Everest was as treacherous and challenging as people make it sound. For starters, ninety per cent of those who attempt the summit ultimately fail. The journey up the south face of the mountain is a gruelling obstacle course that begins with a jumble of ice boulders of varying sizes, and such a trek requires months, if not years, of training. On top of that, there are countless ways for the mountain to take your life. You could fall through an ice shelf, you could experience a cerebral oedema, an avalanche could bury you alive. The list goes on. Yes, Erik attempting to climb Everest would be courageous, but it would also be crazy. And so his dream remained unspoken. Until one day, an acquaintance named Pasquale Scaturro approached Erik and asked him if he would consider climbing Everest along with a team. Pasquale, who had led a successful expedition up Mount Everest before, knew what a skilled climber Erik was, and he also knew that no blind man had ever attempted the highest summit in the world. After giving it a lot of thought along with Ellie and after weighing all the risks, Erik went back to Pasquale with an enthusiastic yes.

Together, Pasquale and Erik recruited a team of veteran climbers, including some of Erik's friends that he had been climbing alongside for years. Since Pasquale had summited Everest before, he served as Erik's coach as he trained. And as Erik trained, he also appealed to organizations and corporations in search of sponsorship.

In the spring of 2001, after two years of planning and preparation, Erik began his ascent of Mount Everest along with Pasquale and the team. The actual expedition began in earnest at a stretch of Himalayan glacier some 18,000 feet above sea level. This section is known as the Khumbu Icefall, and it can make or break an expedition. Getting up the mountain is all about timing: while you have to climb safely, you also have to climb quickly in order to beat the weather.

Pasquale had estimated that the journey across the ice shelf would take the team seven hours at the most. But because Erik was struggling to make it over and around the jumble of icy boulders, it took the team thirteen hours. By the time Erik arrived at Camp 1 (there are four camps before the final push to the summit), his body was beaten and his ego was bruised. As his fellow climbers took note of how long it had taken them, Erik could hear the doubt creeping into their voices—if they didn't go faster, they would never summit. One team member actually suggested carrying Erik's gear up for him, lightening Erik's load so he could move faster. But Erik wouldn't hear it. He had to be an integral member of the team. As he says, he didn't want to be carried to the summit and spiked like a football.

As he recovered in his tent at Camp 1, Erik felt demoralized. He was so sure he could make it to the top, but now reality was slapping him in the face like a gale force wind. He had started in on this expedition with the hope that he could shatter the expectations of what a blind person could do; and now that hope felt like it would be nothing more than an unfulfilled wish.

Erik never really found the maxim "seeing is believing" extremely helpful. Instead, he and his fellow climbers reworked the phrase to something more useful to them and their endeavours: "Believing is seeing." In effect, it means that in order to achieve a desired goal, one must first believe that it's possible. For Erik, this sentiment was never more important than when he was sitting in that tent at the first camp, doubting that he would ever touch the summit. If he was going to make it to the top, Erik had to fundamentally believe that it was possible. He had to envision himself up there. Erik forced himself to sweep aside all of his doubt, as well as everyone else's expectations of him, and he just focused his mind on creating that image of him, standing atop the summit. Once he was able to believe he could do it, he recommitted himself to finishing the expedition with the rest of the team.

Remember how it took Erik thirteen hours to make it across the icefall? Well, since the expedition requires doing that shelf repeatedly in order to get all your gear up to the next camp, Erik had another shot at it. After repeated attempts, Erik managed to cut his time down to five hours. After that, Erik knew he was going to touch the top.

On May 25, 2001, Erik became the first blind person to ever reach the summit of Mount Everest. It felt like the greatest thing Erik could ever accomplish. And yet, once Erik descended the mountain and reached the bottom, Pasquale, his expedition leader, grabbed him by the shoulder and said, "Don't make Everest the greatest thing you ever do."

Can you imagine? A blind man climbs the tallest mountain in the world, and the response he gets is effectively, *"Okay, now what else are you going to do with your life?"* Erik was stunned. But Pasquale wasn't trying to downplay or diminish Erik's accomplishment. Instead, he was hinting at a new lens for Erik's outlook on life. While Erik's feat was highly impressive, it needed to be viewed as part of a greater narrative. Erik needed his journey to be about more than just him. What Erik needed was to hone his *Vision.*

DEFINING VISION

Your Vision is a purpose that inspires you to give your best back to the world. It states who you want to be and why that matters. Your Vision is about more than any single goal or achievement; it is an enduring statement that embodies what you value most. When you read your Vision *statement,* it should ignite a fire inside of you that shouts out, "This is how I plan to live in the world!"

Erik Weihenmayer describes Vision as a guiding light that lives inside of you. When that light is connected to your core values, the light will blaze. For this reason, a big part of discovering and nurturing your Vision involves understanding what matters most to you in your life. It's a self-realization process of finding what fuels that light inside of you. The intent of the Life Element Vision is to guide you in this process of identifying your values and passions. This virtues-based approach will serve as your compass throughout the rest of your journey.

WHY VISION MATTERS

Think about the GPS system in your car or on your phone. It makes traveling from place to place far easier, right? However, it works only if you have an address or coordinates to punch into it. You can't just say, "Tell me my destination." You need to have some idea of where you need to go.

In that same way, Vision will be the coordinates or destination that you're inputting into the GPS of your life. At the moment, you might fall into the Destination Unknown category. That's completely fine because the work you will do here will help you determine the route of your journey.

Research on thousands of No Barriers participants proves that after completing our programs, they know where they're going and what they believe. As one participant stated in their evaluation, "This program has made me a better person and has made me realize why my vision matters." After going through our program, participants consistently state that they "have a clear vision of who I am" and "have a vision that I am passionate about." If you'd like these things in your own life, then learning about Vision should be a top priority for you.

Vision propels you through adversity. It is what keeps you going even when you fail. In your darkest moments, your Vision can serve as the energy that pushes you through your greatest challenges. And it is perhaps THE most critical Life Element because you come back to your Vision over and over again in times of strife.

But you don't have to just take our word for it or the testimonies from our participants. You can also find these concepts in the wisdom of our *Grand Philosophers*. The fundamentals of Vision are steeped in ideas that date back thousands of years, with some of history's greatest thinkers emphasizing the critical significance of purpose as well as its relationship to overcoming adversity.

Grand Philosopher #1
Aristotle

Few philosophers of antiquity worked as tirelessly as Aristotle to understand human existence, especially as it relates to how we should live our lives. His voice is arguably the most lasting and influential on the relationship between purpose and virtue. In Aristotle's estimation, the highest human good was the "activity of the soul in accordance with virtue." He emphasized striving toward your potential based on your unique skills and your deeply held values.

Within the No Barriers model, we adhere closely to these principles, and the Vision element owes a significant debt to one of the Greek philosopher's seminal works, *Nicomachean Ethics*. The text, which is thought to be a compilation of Aristotle's lecture notes from the famed Lyceum, is a key source for the fundamental mission of unleashing our potential and finding that purpose within us. Along with using Vision as a tool to break through adversity, Aristotle talks about Vision as the ultimate aim of humanity.

> *"If happiness is activity in accordance with virtue, it is reasonable that it should be in accordance with the highest virtue; and this will be that of the best thing in us."*

And this connects to another relevant concept that Aristotle explores in the text: *eudaemonism*. The term loosely translates into "happiness," but it's important not to confuse *eudaemonism*'s concept of happiness with our modern interpretation of the word. The essence of *eudaemonism* as Aristotle uses it tries to capture a fuller picture of what it means for humans to fulfil their potential. The broader meaning is intended to characterize a well-lived life. Aristotle was less concerned with the subjective emotional state of *feeling* happy and far more interested in understanding an objective characterization of happiness as it relates to one's virtues. Too often in today's world, we confuse the short-term emotion of happiness with the long-term human need for meaning.

Although research suggests leading a meaningful life and a happy life are related, there are some key differences. In a literature review on the topic, psychologist and author Scott Kaufman, in *Scientific American*, summarizes this important distinction: "It seems that happiness has more to do with having your needs satisfied, getting what you want, and feeling good, whereas meaning is more related to uniquely human activities such as developing a personal identity, expressing the self, and consciously integrating one's past, present, and future experiences."

To draw a clearer distinction between "happiness" and "meaningfulness," let's turn to another one of our Grand Philosophers.

Grand Philosopher #2
Viktor Frankl

In our introduction, we acquainted you with Viktor Frankl and his harrowing personal journey in Nazi Germany, which inspired him to spend the rest of his life studying the relationship between adversity and purpose. He wanted to connect a *why* to the *how* of our human existence. And in his research and analysis—teamed with his own experience as a Holocaust survivor—he began to realize how the notion of happiness fit into that relationship.

As he writes in *Man's Search for Meaning*:

Happiness cannot be pursued; it must ensue, and it only does so as the unintended side-effect of one's personal dedication to a cause greater than oneself or as the by-product of one's surrender to a person other than oneself. Happiness must happen, and the same holds for success: you have to let it happen by not caring about it. I want you to listen to what your conscience commands you to do and go on to carry it out to the best of your knowledge. Then you will live to see that in the long-run—in the long-run, I say!—success will follow you precisely because you had forgotten to think about it.

Think about the first part of that statement for a moment: happiness cannot be *pursued*; instead, happiness *ensues*. For most people, if someone asks them, "What do you want out of life?" they will likely answer, "To be happy." But as Frankl suggests here, it is counterproductive to actively chase after happiness.

And here is why: you cannot control the world around you. Your life is filled with unexpected events that will suddenly strip you of that desired feeling of happiness: the loss of a job, a romantic rejection, the death of a loved one. And if happiness is the one thing you want from life, what do you do in moments like these? How do you endure times of suffering?

Frankl was convinced that while you cannot control the world around you, you can control your response to it. In his own experience, Frankl was intimately acquainted with suffering beyond his control. He was forced into a concentration camp. There, he was tortured, starved of food, and subjected to daily dehumanization. On top of this, he suffered the loss of his wife and family. Happiness was not a choice that was offered to him. Instead, the only thing Frankl could choose was his attitude toward the world. And he decided that he would see life as a challenge to overcome, rather than an endless pursuit of happiness.

Once he made that choice, he was able to find meaning in the suffering. As he said, "In some ways suffering ceases to be suffering at the moment it finds a meaning, such as the meaning of a sacrifice."

As you can see, Frankl's experience, and his ideas that grew from it, is the closest testimony to why Vision is so fundamental to breaking through adversity. His notion that happiness follows meaning, and not the other way around, is a critical element you must consider as you explore what Vision means to you.

But before we ask you to roll up your sleeves and craft a **Vision Statement**, let's underline the other key truth in Frankl's quote above. In discussing the source of happiness, Frankl states that it is "the unintended side-effect of one's personal dedication to a cause greater than oneself."

A cause greater than oneself.

Write this down on a piece of scrap paper or a Post-it note. Now stick it on your fridge. Or, even better, use it as a bookmark as you read through this book. We believe that it is an essential part of what it means to live a purpose-driven life. By seeking to serve a cause greater than yourself, you will find meaning and, through that meaning, happiness.

Remember when Erik reached the top of Mount Everest and Pasquale told him not to let it be the greatest thing he ever did? This is what he was talking about: the significance of linking your purpose to something bigger than yourself. And as you move through the Life Elements in the coming chapters, you will notice that this is a theme we return to over and over again.

Now as you start to think about what your own Vision might look like, let's see how others have practiced Vision in their lives.

VISION IN PRACTICE
Oprah Winfrey

Perhaps no other celebrity speaks about the importance of Vision more eloquently than Oprah Winfrey. She has built a global persona that is all about living a life of purpose. Her personal journey is a living testament to the power of Vision—a Vision she had as a young child.

Oprah grew up in the 50s on a small Mississippi farm with her grandmother. At a time when there were very limited opportunities for African American women, Oprah's Vision was to be more than even her own family would dream possible. Here's how Oprah describes the spark of her revelation:

> I vividly remember standing on my grandmother's small screened-in back porch, churning butter while she boiled clothes in a big black cast-iron pot in the yard. As she pulled the steaming clothes from the pot to hang on the line to dry, she called to me, "Oprah Gail, you better watch me now, 'cause one day you gon' have to know how to do this for yourself."

Yet, even as a small child, Oprah had a gut feeling that there was something else out there. She couldn't quite put her finger on it. She says it was less a voice and more a feeling. In her own words, there was a fire inside of her that said, "This will not be your life. Your life will be more than hanging clothes on a line." Her Vision was to be her very best self, and she knew that meant more than what her grandmother had in mind.

Though there were hints of how that Vision might manifest itself (at the age of three, she was known as the "little speaker" for her ability to recite poetry), she couldn't have known that the path she would ultimately take would impact hundreds of millions of lives. Living first with her grandmother, then her mother, and eventually her father, she did not have a stable childhood. Yet, as she says, "My entire life experience, my ability to believe in myself and even in my darkest moments of sexual abuse and being physically abused, and so forth, I knew there was another way." Ultimately, it was her father's love that enabled her to flourish. From her first job at age nineteen as a co-news anchor at Nashville's CBS affiliate, WTVF-TV, she would ascend quickly to one of the most recognized leaders the world has ever known.

Importantly, Oprah's early Vision was *not* a specific goal. It was a gut feeling that she could be something more than anyone thought possible. Her childhood *goal* was to be a teacher. And that goal still rings true for her. Asked about what she'd do if she could go back and do it all over again, she says, "I would definitely, definitely, definitely be teaching in a classroom. It's the thing that still brings me the greatest joy."

But Oprah's Vision was more enduring than any one step on her incredible journey. She might reframe her Vision now as a desire to fulfil the highest, truest expression of herself. Humbly, she continues to look back at her career and think, though she's successful, she has not fully manifested that Vision. Her Vision continues to drive her.

CarrieAnn Mathis

Vision is a powerful thing, and it can be scary. But it doesn't always lead to becoming a billionaire media executive and globally renowned celebrity.

Army veteran CarrieAnn Mathis is one of millions of veterans who suffer from post-traumatic stress disorder. Like many veterans, she struggled to find community, purpose, and identity after her military service. The mental obstacles warriors often confront when returning home can seem as insurmountable as physical injuries. In her own words, Mathis felt stuck in her post-military life due to limitations she had placed on herself. She was stifled by expectations others had of what her life should be. She knew she had to make a change but was struggling to find the courage to put her finger on what exactly she envisioned for her future.

Then came No Barriers. Mathis enrolled in a No Barriers Veteran Wilderness Expedition—a week of self-reflection and whitewater rafting with fellow veterans.

There was just one problem: "I was deathly afraid of dark water," admits Mathis. "There was always this feeling of being trapped and not being able to escape. That metaphor had a closer meaning to my life, which I discovered during the expedition."

Going into her expedition, Mathis knew that she could use some help to overcome her fears. Much like the army, it required a team effort. "I cried every day on the boat," she says, drawing a comparison to her struggle with PTSD. "The rapids were the hardest part for me, not because they were dangerous, but because I could not control them."

Determined to confront her fear, Mathis opted out of the "regular boat" option, where the participants could simply ride without tackling the rapids. Instead, she decided to paddle through the crushing waters, not just for herself but for her team. "Everyone is responsible for not drowning everyone else," she says.

By the end, she even "rode the bull," sitting at the front of the paddle boat and holding onto a rope through the full force of the rapids. Mathis describes that as her "best day on the journey."

On many of our No Barriers programs, we ask participants at the end of their experience to take a personal **pledge**. The pledge is a commitment to move something important forward in their life. Some pledge to craft their Vision. Others pledge a Reach goal related to physical, mental, or emotional fitness. We often put our pledges on a physical object—the No Barriers Flag—so that we can have a visual reminder of the commitments we made in the midst of our programmatic experiences.

Near the end of Mathis' experience, she finally found the courage to define an enduring Vision for herself. She encapsulated it in a single phrase: "Live a life of peace and strength in the mountains."

Living that Vision required her to get out of a relationship, sell her house in Texas, and move to Colorado. When we commit to our Vision, it's not choosing the easy path; it's committing to live a life of purpose no matter what comes in our way.

As Mathis describes it:

I felt free and scared at the same time when I accomplished my pledge. I had done it: quit my job, sold my house, and moved to the mountains. There was definitely a grieving process that went along with accomplishing my pledge. I was grieving the life I thought I had, was supposed to have, or thought I should have had. I had moved on my own and didn't have a definite outcome. I had always made the safe decision in life where I knew there was security. At the same time, I was living with barriers and not being who I needed to be. The move gave me peace with who I was and where I should be. It's a decision I have been wanting to make for years but never had the guts to do it.

So, you've seen how others practice Vision in their lives. Now, here comes the hard part: creating your own Vision. Are you ready?

CREATING YOUR VISION

It's time for you to embark on your epic quest for purpose and meaning. And the first step in that journey is writing out your Vision Statement. But before you put pen to paper, it's helpful to quickly consider what Vision *is not*; in doing so, hopefully you can avoid some of the missteps that many people make when initially trying to work through their Vision.

For starters, Vision *is not* about seeing the future. As discussed earlier, life is unpredictable and you will not be able to forecast every beat of your as-yet untold story. With that in mind, your Vision should remain broad enough that it will help you overcome an array of challenges that you might confront in life.

Second, Vision *is not* an unchanging thing. Your statement that you write will not be encased in amber, never to be revised. Part of being human is being adaptable. The concept of Vision allows room for you to change and grow, so you do not need to stress out about making it perfect.

Last and perhaps most importantly for this exercise, Vision *is not* a list of goals. This is the most common misconception we come across. Defining your Vision is a qualitative endeavour, not a quantitative one. We are not asking you to create a bucket list for you to check off over the course of your life.

Since the distinction between Vision and Goals is the branch people trip over most often in our programs, we want to make sure we draw the contrast as clearly as possible as you get going.

UNDERSTANDING THE DIFFERENCE BETWEEN VISION AND GOALS

Getting the scope right in your Vision Statement will be important. For Vision, you are not identifying a goal. You are creating a statement that clearly states your values and passions.

The examples below demonstrate how we differentiate between a vision and a goal.

Vision	Goal
I am more physically fit, serving as a role model to my children to live a healthy and happy life.	Run a 10K.
I share my strengths with my community through service and outreach.	Do two hours of community service every week.
I have a job that leverages my unique talents.	Assess my strengths and determine how my current role aligns.

Vision	Goal
I am integrating the things that I love most into my everyday activities. This includes dancing, singing, reading, and laughing.	Try a new dance class.

Do you see the difference? The Vision column is a values-focused statement that allows you to still feel the reward and enrich your life even if the specific goal is not achieved. If I train for a 10K but ultimately cannot finish the 10K, I am still healthier and happier because I imbued the journey of the goal with meaning.

CLARIFYING YOUR VALUES

David Brooks famously asks in a 2014 TED Talk, "Are you living for your resume or for your eulogy?" Here, Brooks is prompting the audience to consider the different virtues we emphasize through these two separate lenses. In the framework of a resume, you are more often thinking about a list of tangible accomplishments—your academic achievements, your career milestones, and awards that may have been bestowed upon you. Whereas, through the lens of an imagined eulogy, you are likely more focused on the things you want people to remember you for—the depth of your character, the strength of your convictions, or maybe your loyalty as a friend or spouse. In this question that Brooks poses, "resume" is shorthand for external success, and "eulogy" represents internal values.

Now, by no means are we suggesting that it is wrong to be focused on your resume virtues; in fact, many people's careers are deeply intertwined with their identities. But we want you to consider which of these lenses you rely on the most as you begin thinking about your own values. It is okay to want external success, but as we emphasize at No Barriers, that external success is far more fulfilling if it is driven by internal values.

Maybe for you, the answer to Brooks's question seems obvious. You have worked hard to make choices in life aligned with your personal values. Or maybe the question feels big and overwhelming. Or perhaps you feel as though life's many demands have kept you from making decisions based on your values.

(If that last feeling strongly resonates with you, don't fret. This book will break the process down into smaller, achievable steps.)

So, here's a quick gut check. To determine if you are aligning yourself with your values, ask yourself the following questions:

- What inspires you and gets you up in the morning?
- What are the things that bring you joy?
- What activities, experiences, and people help you feel grounded and connected to your life?

And now for two big, important questions:

- What do you need to let go of (values, beliefs, behaviours) to integrate your answers to the questions above into your daily routines?
- How big of a change are you willing to make to integrate your answers to the questions above into your daily routines?

Many of us do not have the luxury of quitting our jobs and moving to a tropical island because the sounds of ocean waves make us happy. So being realistic with yourself about your commitment to change is an important step in being more intentional about integrating your values into your day-to-day activities.

And here's another tip: *go for clarity, then action.*

If you have not yet taken the time to identify your values, this is the time to do it. Write down a list of your values that serve as guidelines for your day-to-day decision making.

Sample values include:

Trust	Respect	Independence
Compassion	Excellence	Good Health
Leadership	Adventure	Curiosity
Kindness	Humour	Gratitude

As you consider your values, you may find this quote from Russ Harris, acclaimed author of *The Happiness Trap*, helpful in sorting through your thoughts:

Values are your heart's deepest desires for how you want to behave as a human being. Values are not about what you want to get or achieve; they are about how you want to behave or act on an ongoing basis.

FIND YOUR FUEL

Now, as you begin to shape your list of core values into a Vision Statement, keep in mind that the best Vision is one that holds plenty of potential energy. Within the words of your Vision Statement, there should be implicit action—things for you to do.

Look at this Vision Statement from the examples above: *I share my strengths with my community through service and outreach.* Putting these words into action might involve adopting a highway, or heading up a clothing drive, or coaching in a youth soccer league, or maybe singing in your church choir.

You also want to ensure that the statement is defined by your passions. What is going to get you out of bed in the morning? What is going to keep you going?

Let's look at another Vision Statement from our examples: *I am integrating the things I love most into my everyday activities. That includes dancing, singing, reading, and laughing.* If these are all things you love to do, just imagine how much easier it will be for you to live out your Vision Statement and gain meaning.

Also, remember that you can think about your Vision within a variety of contexts: work, family, relationships, health, personal performance, or all of the above. It's up to you to decide what would be most impactful to you at this particular point in time.

TAKE A FIRST STEP

This is the part where we tell you it's okay to fail. We get it: the blank page in front of you can be a daunting thing. What we're asking of you is not meant to be easy.

Even though we all want to "just know" what we're supposed to do with our lives, for our purpose to be spelled out for us, that's not how a calling works. And that's exactly what Vision is—it's a *calling*.

We have guided thousands of people just like you through this process. It's never clear and hardly ever obvious, especially when you're starting out. You want it to come all at once, and you feel frustrated when that doesn't happen. But when you start to take those first steps, when you commit to some course of action, you begin to see what was there all along.

Here's the other thing to remember: Vision can be a bit of an ongoing dance. You might think you have nailed your Vision Statement here, but as you go through the other Life Elements, they might spark emotions and objectives you hadn't thought of yet. You can then adapt your Vision Statement to those new ideas. Alternatively, maybe you feel stuck right now, and you just can't express your Vision in a way that's satisfying. Do not worry. There is no need to force it. Instead, continue on in the book, submerse yourself in the other Life Elements, and come back to crafting your statement when you're ready. The principles you learn in subsequent chapters can actually help you hone your Vision.

AFTER THE PEAK

The day after Erik Weihenmayer climbed down from that snowy, windblown mountaintop on Everest, he was confronted by a new kind of storm—the whirlwind of fame. After years of climbing under the radar, suddenly Erik's face was on billboards, he was featured on the cover of *Time* magazine, he was interviewed on *Oprah*. His seemingly impossible feat would be documented in the film *Farther than the Eye Can See* as well as a TV movie, *Touch the Top*. Erik's story was powerful and inspiring, and people wanted to hear it.

To the outside world, Erik had achieved it all. And yet, he couldn't shake the feeling that something was missing. As Pasquale's words echoed in his head—*"Don't make Everest the greatest thing you ever do"*—Erik realized the deeper meaning that his friend was trying to relay: "I didn't want my life to be a conquest. Goals feel like false summits; you reach what you thought was the top, only to discover a higher summit. So, you continue to climb higher and higher, always finding another summit a little higher, and you never find what you're looking for. The magic of life has to exist beyond a perpetual series of summits."

As Erik was contemplating what was missing from his life, he thought back to a time when he still had just a tiny bit of his sight remaining in his right eye—a time when, if he pressed his face against the screen, he could still watch television. In those waning days just before he went blind completely, he saw a news program that was focused on a young man named Terry Fox. Terry was a Canadian who had lost one of his legs to cancer, and he was in the hospital when he decided he was going to run across Canada in order to raise awareness for the disease. This would entail running thousands of miles, essentially a marathon per day, and he would be doing it on a rudimentary prosthetic. As the young Erik struggled to see Terry's unbelievable feat unfold on screen, he caught a glimpse of Terry's face, and in it, Erik saw a light. It was this internal light that seemed to be fuelling him. And that's what Erik decided he wanted—a purpose that would fuel him through the tough times.

Erik set to work on crafting his own Vision. For him, it was a process of first reckoning with his internal landscape, understanding what mattered most to him, and then putting his values into action. What the process revealed to Erik was that he valued leadership and community, and he was fuelled by adventure that is shared with others. Here's the Vision Statement he crafted:

> To find a way to lead despite my own fears, to push myself beyond my understanding of what I'm capable of, and to always be a good partner and friend.

He also realized that his feats could build awareness for the blind community and the disabled community at large; and, in doing so, he could grow the confidence within that community. But it goes beyond that, too. As he considered his own journey, he realized that all of us feel like we're climbing blind at times. For him, no matter a person's ability or disability, we all face adversities; we are all in need of a map to help guide us through our challenges.

Once Erik's goals became an outgrowth of his Vision, his adventures took on greater meaning in his life. Since that day in May 2001, when Erik stood in the wind at the top of Mount Everest, he has not stopped attempting remarkable feats. Several years after Everest, Erik completed the Seven Summits, putting him in yet another exclusive club. He has also taken on skydiving, caving, marathon running, and even kayaking. (In fact, Erik recently kayaked the entire 277 miles of the Grand Canyon.)

But even though Erik has become one of the most celebrated athletes in the world, he has not lost sight of his Vision, which grew out of his need for a universal human experience. Today, Erik spends his time speaking to organizations and corporations, using his own life experiences to help others draw their own maps.

"My heart burned with the memory of my heroes, people like Helen Keller, who took the world's perceptions about the disabled and shattered them into a million pieces, people whose stories made me hunger for the courage to live in their image."

—Erik Weihenmayer

CHAPTER TWO

Reach

**"A journey of a thousand miles
begins with a single step."**
—Lao Tzu

MUSIC IN THE SILENCE

When Mandy Harvey arrived at Colorado State University for her freshman year of college, she showed up with a few duffels of clothes, her guitar, and a dream: she was going to become a music teacher. Everything up to that moment had prepared her for this. Mandy had been singing and playing music since the age of four—oftentimes recording tunes with her father, who played the guitar. Through years of study and training, she had developed perfect pitch. In her senior year of high school, her class had voted her Best Vocalist. And along with an all-star high school chorus, Mandy had travelled to Australia, where she sang at the revered Concert Hall at the Sydney Opera House. So, when she got into her top-choice music program at CSU, her fingers were tingling with the sense that her dream was now within reach.

But within two months of Mandy matriculating at CSU, she noticed something strange and unsettling: she was having trouble hearing her professors during class. Even when she tried moving closer to the front of the lecture halls, her struggle to hear remained. This was not normal for Mandy. Moreover, her ears constantly felt like they needed to pop—like that feeling you get at the beginning of a flight when the plane is taking off—only for Mandy, that uncomfortable sensation wouldn't subside. Finally, she decided she needed to see an audiologist to find out what was going on with her hearing.

The doctor's assessment was distressing. Mandy had lost forty decibels of her hearing ability. This put her at the high end of what is considered *mild* hearing loss. (*Moderate* hearing loss falls between 41 dB and 70 dB; *severe* hearing loss is between 71 dB and 90 dB; while *profound* hearing loss happens when people have lost more than 90 dB.) According to the audiologist, the nerves inside Mandy's ears were deteriorating due to Ehlers-Danlos syndrome (EDS), a rare genetic disorder that affects the connective tissue throughout a person's body. People with EDS can experience stretchy skin, overly flexible joints, and shifting organs, among other things. For Mandy, EDS was also affecting her auditory system. This meant that when sound waves reached her ear, the sound often had trouble being conducted from her middle ear to her inner ear.

While the doctor's diagnosis was difficult for Mandy to hear, the prognosis was impossible for her to comprehend. There was a strong chance that Mandy's hearing loss was irreversible. Even worse, the nerve deterioration would likely continue. And when the audiologist prescribed hearing aids for Mandy to use, they proved to be an ineffective solution. Hearing aids amplify the hearing a person has, and since Mandy's hearing was on the way out, they were helpful for only a short time.

Having lost 40 dB of her hearing meant that although Mandy could do reasonably well in one-on-one conversations with people, she would miss words when talking on the phone or in places with more than the usual background noise. And, of course, it meant that Mandy would struggle to hear all the subtle notes and tones in musical compositions.

This presented obvious problems for her in the music program at CSU. If she couldn't fully hear the music, how could she sing on key? How could she stay at tempo with her fellow musicians? Ultimately, how could she perform at the high level that her professors and peers expected? In some classes, she was required to learn difficult pieces of music just from a recording with no sheet music permitted. Even if a gifted music student had pristine hearing, this could be challenging. For Mandy, it became a herculean task.

But Mandy refused to quit. For a time, she kept showing up to class and pretending that she could still hear. She knew this was an unsustainable solution that was born, at least in part, out of a need to deny it was actually happening. But she didn't know what else to do: music had been her dream. It was who she was, and she refused to let anything stop her from pursuing it.

As fall turned to winter and winter to spring, Mandy's hearing continued to deteriorate. In her 2017 memoir titled, *Sensing the Rhythm*, Mandy refers to this period as her "descent into silence." During her second semester at CSU, Mandy was so painfully aware of the sounds that were disappearing from her everyday life that she started to carry around a notebook to jot down things she could no longer hear. First, the twitter of birds, then the patter of rain, the whisper of a windy day, and even the laughter of friends and family. It was as if the natural world around her was a symphony orchestra, and a conductor was silencing each instrument in that world one by one until no music remained.

Another cherished thing Mandy was losing forever was all the songs and albums that had created the soundtrack to her young life. There was Tegan and Sara's *So Jealous*, The Killers' *Hot Fuss*, Ryan Adams's *Gold*, Thirty Seconds to Mars's *A Beautiful Life*. There were the jazz standards she had performed, and the operas she had studied. There was Harry Nilsson, and the Association, and America; music of the 60s and 70s she inherited from her father. And then there was Charlie Chaplin's *Smile*—a song she was determined to sing over and over again in those final months until it was tattooed on her heart so that it would be with her always, even after her hearing was no longer there.

Mandy would lie on the floor of her college dorm room with a pair of Bose headphones on, and she would blast the music into her ears for hours on end. If you ask Mandy whether she can remember the last album she ever listened to before her hearing slipped into oblivion, she answers without hesitation: My Chemical Romance's *Black Parade*. She was down to her last few decibels of hearing as the angsty sound waves of the glam-goth band fought to make it to her inner ears. The title track of the album seems fitting as it brims with darker emotions and its increasingly desperate beat. Mandy may not have been able to hear the words that the lead singer, Gerard Way, was belting out, but he could have been singing about her in that very moment: *"And in my heart I can't contain it/ The anthem won't explain it/ A world that sends you reeling/ From decimated dreams."*

That final song for Mandy was like a dirge, both in its melancholic tone and in the symbolic resonance it held for Mandy. As Mandy has said of that last gasp of her hearing, "I died that day."

As you can imagine, Mandy slipped into a deep depression that lasted more than a year. To her, it felt like she had fallen down a dark well. After she was dropped from the music program at CSU at the end of her freshman year, she moved home with her parents. There, she hid from the world, shutting out friends and family. She got a job working remotely from home, doing the billing for a local rheumatology practice twenty hours a week. The rest of her time was spent grieving the loss of her hearing or coping with her newfound fears. Now that Mandy was *profoundly* deaf, she developed a crippling fear of the dark. While most people have at least a mild fear of the dark, they have the advantage of being able to hear if anything is lurking in that darkness. For Mandy, that was a tool she no longer had. And so this led to another fear—losing her sight. If Mandy could no longer *hear* or *see*, how would she be able to function in the world? (This is not an uncommon fear in the deaf and the blind communities; once you have lost one of your senses, it's that much more believable that you will lose another.)

So, Mandy was depressed. She was alone. And her life was hemmed in by fear.

And then something happened—something unexpected and life changing. One day, Mandy's father came to her and suggested they go to the basement and record a song together, just as they had done so many times before when she was younger. "Are you willing to take a risk and find a new song to sing?" he asked her. Mandy thought her father was nuts. *How was she going to sing or play music if she couldn't hear?* Reluctantly, Mandy agreed to try, if only to prove to her father that it would never work.

That day, Mandy sat down with a visual tuner, a small device that tells you precisely what note you're singing or playing. (Once you hit the note exactly, a light on the tuner flashes green.) She spent eight straight hours singing into that tuner, feeling how each note resonated within her as the tuner flashed green. With the help of muscle memory and all her years of training, Mandy was able to find her middle C and then move up and down the scale from there. When she was satisfied that she could sing each note, she sat with her father and attempted to lay down a track with him.

As she began singing, Mandy noticed tears forming in her father's eyes. Her first thought was that she had failed—badly. Her heart sank. She couldn't hear the notes herself, so she was depending on her father's reaction, and to her, his face registered disappointment. But then he signed to her, telling her that the tears were tears of joy. She had perfect pitch. She was relieved and filled with new hope.

Mandy chose a song that day she had never heard before, one that she knew was a favourite of her sister's: One Republic's *Come Home*. And as Mandy sang from the sheet music and her father accompanied her, that's exactly what that moment felt like to her—coming home.

Not long after Mandy recorded that song with her father, she played the recording for her former vocal coach. And the vocal coach couldn't believe her own ears. In fact, she was so impressed that she encouraged Mandy to perform at a local jazz venue, Jay's Bistro. While Mandy was still uncertain in her abilities, she agreed to try it—just as she had agreed to try recording a song with her father.

That first night back on a stage since she had lost her hearing, Mandy stood there in front of the small crowd in

Jay's Bistro and sang *My Funny Valentine*. By keeping her hand on the piano as the pianist played, Mandy could feel the rhythm and cues through the vibrations of the notes. If Mandy had not told the crowd she was deaf, they may never have known. She finished the song to applause from the crowd; and at the end of the evening, the owner came to her and asked Mandy to return to the venue and play a full set.

For Mandy, she had found her voice again. She began playing regularly at Jay's Bistro. She started recording albums, singing covers of old jazz standards. And she was even invited to perform at the hallowed Kennedy Center in Washington, DC. And yet . . .

Mandy still felt like something was missing in her journey back from losing her hearing. As she says of that moment in her life, "Coming back to music was personal, but it didn't heal me." For her, this wasn't where her healing ended, as one might think. Instead, it's where her healing began. Although she was singing again—and finding success in doing it—Mandy still felt unfulfilled. She wanted to know why.

DEFINING REACH

Very simply, Reach is seeking opportunities to step outside your comfort zone and achieve your full potential. It's a process of going off script from what you normally might do. In this Life Element, you will embrace any kind of adversity that is present in your life right now and choose to use it as a way to grow. To put it another way, Reach is about finding the verbs to go with your Vision Statement. What *actions* are you going to take to move you closer to your defined purpose?

Think about Mandy Harvey's story so far in the context of Reach. Making that decision to record a song with her father—that was a Reach moment. It took her completely out of her comfort zone; but through that process, she planted the seeds to a new future for herself. And what followed? She met with her old voice coach, who encouraged Mandy to sing in public. Another Reach moment. While Mandy didn't know it at the time, she was taking small steps that would start her on the path to an unbelievable journey (as you will see at the end of this chapter). And she made it possible by being open to embracing the adversity in her life.

The same could be said of Erik Weihenmayer, who was making small, achievable Reaches—wrestling, climbing, starting an organization—in order to discover that next hold in the rock wall of his journey. In our No Barriers community, we often use the language of climbing a mountain to describe this journey ahead of you, and with Reach, it is especially helpful. While climbing, you are always reaching for the next hold, not always knowing where it will be. You know you're trying to get to the top, but you only get there by constantly reaching, one stretch at a time.

But as you read through the pages ahead, keep in mind that Reach goes much further than claiming an ambitious goal for yourself. It can't just be framed as checking a box off a list of to-dos. That rarely works. Just think of New Year's resolutions.

According to *US News & World Report*, eighty per cent of the resolutions you make on New Year's Eve fail by February. While it differs from person to person, it's telling that we, as a society, are not good at carrying out what we resolve to do, even after one month. What exactly goes wrong in this process?

Part of the challenge may be that when we make a New Year's resolution, it is not closely connected to our individual Vision. Or even if the resolution is aligned with our Vision, maybe the resolution is too big of a step or too intimidating and outside of our comfort zone. You need to find ways to break down your ambition into manageable pieces. You know how they say you eat an elephant? One bite at a time.

The other challenging aspect is that we make it an all-or-nothing proposition. You know that feeling you get when you slip up for the first time with your New Year's resolution? You feel like you failed, so then you simply toss in the towel on the resolution altogether. That sort of defeatist attitude is unhelpful. Instead, you need to allow yourself to see failing as just another step along your journey. Reach isn't about getting it exactly right every time. As the saying goes, don't let the perfect be the enemy of the good.

In this chapter, you will use your Vision Statement to help you determine how you can step outside of your comfort zone in order to learn and grow. You will look around you and identify the adversities in your life. Those adversities could be in the form of a challenging project at work, or a broken relationship that needs mending, or even that continuing education class to which you keep promising to apply. We want you to dig deep and name that adversity that you have been putting off because it's time to begin the process of moving from your Vision, to identifying your Reach, to naming the smallest, most achievable first step.

WHY REACH MATTERS

You've seen inspirational quotes that encourage you to achieve your goals and reach outside your comfort zone, to do something you wouldn't normally do; but getting out of your routine can ask a lot of you. Your comfort zone is a space where your activities and behaviours fit a routine and pattern that minimizes stress and risk. It provides a state of mental security, and you benefit in obvious ways—regular happiness, low anxiety, and reduced stress. So, when you try to go outside of that zone, there's a certain amount of risk involved, and oftentimes it can leave you feeling vulnerable. In addition, leaving your comfort zone can amplify your anxiety. But the process of Reach, as we have conceived it, shows you how vulnerability and the right level of anxiety can be a plus in your search for purpose.

There's actually a lot of science that explains why it's so hard to break out of your comfort zone and why it's good for you when you do it. The idea of the comfort zone goes back to a classic experiment in psychology. Back in 1908, psychologists Robert M. Yerkes and John D. Dodson explained that a state of relative comfort created a steady level of performance. In order to maximize performance, however, we need a state of relative anxiety—a space where our stress levels are slightly higher than normal. This space is called *Optimal Anxiety*, and it's just outside our comfort zone. Too little anxiety, and we underperform; too much anxiety, and we become too stressed to be productive, and our performance drops off sharply.

Anyone who's ever pushed themselves to get to the next level or accomplish something difficult knows that when you really challenge yourself, you can turn up amazing results. More than a few studies support the point. However, pushing *too* hard can actually cause a negative result and reinforce the mental construct that challenging yourself is a bad idea. It's our natural tendency to return to an anxiety-neutral, comfortable state. You can understand why it's so hard to kick your brain out of your comfort zone.

But the truth is, you miss out on so much in life just by not raising your hand, your voice, or your platform. With that in mind, here are the top five reasons to step outside your comfort zone:

1. ***Opportunity to grow.*** Challenging yourself can help you be your best self and unleash your fullest potential. We aren't finished products, and

in order to be our best selves, we need to step outside our comfort zone in order to level up. You can't expect to reach new heights if you only stick to your same thinking and routine.

2. *Learn about yourself.* Stepping outside your comfort zone will help you know yourself at a deeper level. It will inform you about your interests, passions, talents, strengths, and weaknesses even if some of them have been hidden. Every time you reach for something you didn't think you were capable of, you become more informed, knowledgeable, and skilled.

3. *Increase your self-confidence.* Embracing the unknown and proving to yourself that you can push past your barriers helps to build your self-confidence and self-esteem. Your insecurity will grow every time you pass up an opportunity to try something. On the other hand, your confidence will be fuelled every time that you try. If you stop thinking and start trying, you will realize what's possible.

4. *Learn to deal with challenges.* Life is unpredictable and it's important to have the skills and confidence to face them head-on. Knowing that you are able to overcome something outside your comfort zone will build your confidence and reinforce your sense of independence.

5. *Build deeper relationships.* Trying something new often opens up opportunities to connect with

people in deeper ways that might not have been available if you remained in your comfort zone. When we take risks, we are being vulnerable to the chance we may fail. It's often during these times when we are trying to push past our barriers that we depend on and feel the support of others—sometimes friends and sometimes strangers. It's during these moments that we connect in a deeper way with others.

As you can see, practicing Reach by stretching outside of your comfort zone can have a halo effect on your life, empowering you in unexpected ways. The trick is to take it one Reach at a time, going just a little bit further and then a little bit further, until you've attained that optimal anxiety. In doing so, you will help to transform your lift and move closer to your Vision.

In our own research on Reach within the No Barriers community, ninety per cent to ninety-six per cent of our participants agree or strongly agree with the following statements after their programs: "I want to reach for my potential" and "It is important to get outside my comfort zone." This is a growth of twenty per cent to forty per cent on average compared to what participants say before entering the program.

Just as important, more than eighty per cent say that they "know how to take the first step towards reaching my potential." Or, as this participant put in his own words, "I feel like I can go outside my comfort zone to grow and reach my goals. I believe in myself more than I used to."

Whether you're already at ease with stretching outside your comfort zone to grow and develop or you need to believe that it is possible, the stories and tools in this chapter will help you become an expert at Reaching into the unknown.

Now, let's turn to a few more of our Grand Philosophers as we do a closer examination of the foundations of the Reach element.

Grand Philosopher #1
Lao Tzu

Lao Tzu is a major figure in Chinese philosophy, a sage of the sixth century who is traditionally thought of as one of the founding voices of Taoism, which focuses on the search for harmony with the forces of the universe. Over the centuries since Lao Tzu's time, the legendary philosopher has served as an inspiration to people across the globe who seek balance in their lives.

As with most other ancient Chinese thinkers, Lao Tzu's way of explaining his ideas often uses paradox, analogy, appropriation of ancient sayings, repetition, symmetry, rhyme, and rhythm. The writings attributed to him are poetical and dense, but they resonate with concepts that have surpassed the test of time. One of his most often pinned quotes is, "A journey of a thousand miles begins with a single step." This famous line, pulled from the sixty-fourth verse of the *Tao Te Ching*, highlights the idea that great things start from humble beginnings. (Interestingly, in the original version, the text refers to *"1,000 li journey."* A *li* is an old Chinese measure of distance, which converts to 360 miles or 576 kilometres.)

The heart of this verse reminds us that in order to change, you don't need to stress about the entire journey that lies ahead of you. Instead, all we need to do to change is take the first step. It is often the hardest step, but once it is taken, those that follow become easier. It also reminds us that we can't go back and do over what is already done. All we ever have is now, this moment.

The same applies in No Barriers's Reach element. Sometimes it's a process of trial and error, which implies that you may fail; and when you do, it's important to not let those moments keep you from moving forward. We want you to concentrate only on doing the next right thing that is in the direction of your Vision. One step, one moment, one day at a time is the way of the Tao; it's also the recommended practice of Reach.

Grand Philosopher #2
Andy Molinsky

Andy Molinsky literally wrote the book on Reach. He is a professor at Brandeis University's International Business School and a contributor to business publications such as *Forbes*. In 2017, Molinsky published *REACH: A New*

Strategy to Help You Step outside Your Comfort Zone, Rise to the Challenge, and Build Confidence.

In the book, Molinsky explores what it means to reach beyond your comfort zone, and he outlines a set of reasons for why it can be so hard for us to do so. Once you recognize these reasons, you can start to develop a plan for addressing them.

For a moment, think about a time in recent memory when you wanted to go outside of your comfort zone, but then something stopped you. What was it that kept you from reaching? Can you remember?

Most likely, it was a psychological barrier. Somewhere in the back of your mind, there was a voice that made you doubt the action you were about to take. In response to that voice, you avoided leaving your comfort zone at all.

In Molinsky's book, he lists possible causes for this avoidance. In some cases, perhaps the situation feels inauthentic to who you are. Or maybe you are anxious about how others will respond to the new behaviour you're adopting. In other cases, you believe there's a chance you might fail at your Reach, and the fear of performing poorly keeps you from trying at all. Then in the rarest of cases, maybe your Reach gives you an unsettling feeling—for example, you must fire someone who works for you, or you have to cut a toxic friend out of your life.

These are some of the possible reasons why you avoid Reaching. It can be a single one of these things that blocks you from Reaching or a combination of them. And knowing these reasons can help you identify what's in your way.

So now let's look at ways Molinsky tells you *how* to Reach even with these predictable challenges creating psychological barriers.

For starters, you need **conviction**. You need to believe that there is a profound and justifiable reason for your Reach that will take you out of your comfort zone. Another way to say this? You need to have a legitimate purpose to make all the strain and stress that you will invariably endure worth it. In short, the gain has to be worth the pain. Luckily for you, the Vision that you are crafting for yourself will serve as the source of your conviction. Your Vision will help you focus on *why* you are doing something, rather than focusing on *why not* to do something.

Molinsky also identifies **customization** as an important tool in your toolkit. Reach is not a one-size-fits-all proposition. In many instances, you will need to find your own personal way of performing a task. As an example, maybe you've been promoted to a new management role at work, one that requires you to delegate to others. You've seen the way other managers at the company tersely boss around employees, and that feels uncomfortable for you. Here, you might customize your management style, tailoring it to a demeanour that better fits your personality. You're still going outside of your comfort zone, but you're customizing your approach. You're asking yourself, "How can I make myself feel most comfortable in an uncomfortable situation?"

Clarity is the third and final resource you should incorporate into your Reach moments. Molinsky talks about the importance of maintaining an honest perspective on why you are avoiding a certain task or relationship. This requires genuine introspection on your part as you try to clearly identify the ways in which you're avoiding something, as well as the rationale you're using to make that avoidance acceptable. In short, admitting the problem is the first step in solving it.

It's worth noting that Molinsky has a distinctly business-oriented bent in his philosophies, and his book really leans into personal growth in the workplace. That said, his concepts are applicable to anyone trying to break out of their comfort zone. And since, in the No Barriers community, getting outside that comfort zone is an important part of our Reach process, Molinsky's ideas have informed this particular Life Element. As Molinsky highlights in the book, there's an incredibly powerful effect of simply giving something a try; that's exactly what we're asking you to do in your own personal reach.

Okay, now let's check in on how others have embraced the concepts of Reach in their lives.

REACH IN PRACTICE
Michael Phelps

How do you win twenty-eight Olympic medals? You win them one medal at a time. (Also an acceptable answer: You train like nobody else before you has ever trained.) Michael

Phelps is the most decorated athlete in the history of the Olympic Games. But what's interesting is beyond his intense physical training, such an impressive feat required a lot of specific habit forming from the famed swimmer. For Phelps, it was a cumulation of a bunch of small reaches, which is a key part of practicing this Life Element.

In a way, Phelps fell backward into swimming. His mom was intent on him burning some energy that was creating a headache for his teachers at school. So, she put her seven-year-old son in the pool and had him swim it off. When local swimming coach, Bob Bowman, saw Phelps swimming, the first thing he noticed was Phelps's physique—the long torso with his short legs and big hands—and his gut told him that Phelps could become a champion.

But while Phelps's physique made him a natural, his emotional energy was a problem. Bowman noticed that Phelps had trouble calming down before races, and the coach realized that his training would have to be both physical *and* mental. Bowman zeroed in on a few specific habits that would help pull Phelps out of his comfort zone and put the swimmer into a better mindset for competing. As Charles Duhigg (author of *The Power of Habit*) recalls Bowman saying:

> We'd experiment, try different things until we found stuff that worked. Eventually we figured out it was best to concentrate on these tiny moments of success and build them into mental triggers. We worked them into a routine. There's a series of

things we do before every race that are designed to give Michael a sense of building victory.

As Bowman and Phelps worked closely together on developing habits of visualization and relaxation, they began to see results in Phelps's performance. In swimming, victory can come down to the length of a razor-thin fingernail. Bowman found that small behavioural changes made all the difference. As Phelps turned his small reaches into habits, his heat times came down and his star rose.

At the Beijing Olympics in 2008, Michael Phelps would have to do a literal series of reaches in order to score a medal. At the start of the 200-meter butterfly, Phelps went through his routine of stepping on and off the block, swinging his arms three times, and then taking his stance on the block again. Then the gun sounded, and Phelps and the other swimmers launched into the water. But as soon as Phelps entered the pool, he noticed moisture in his goggles. There was a leak in the seal of the goggles, and that meant his vision would be cloudy throughout the entire race. His only hope was that it wouldn't get worse.

But halfway through the race, the leak did worsen. Suddenly, Phelps's goggles were completely fogged up, impeding his vision almost completely. Talk about being out of one's comfort zone: Phelps was in the middle of an Olympic event, and he couldn't see a thing. However, Phelps remained calm—as cool as the other side of the pillow.

And here's why.

Some years earlier at a training facility in Michigan, Bob Bowman had actually made Phelps swim laps in a pool while the lights were out. The place was pitch dark, and Phelps had to estimate how far out the wall was as he swam blindly. For Bowman, this was another way to ready his swimmer for anything—to mentally prepare Phelps for any moment that might be out of his comfort zone. That reach Phelps made in that darkened pool would now help him when it counted most.

Back in that pool in Beijing at the Olympics, Phelps was now counting out his butterfly strokes—each reach he made with his arms. Because he had trained for this very moment, he could estimate how many strokes he would need to get to the next turn, which would then launch him into the final stretch. In his mind, it was twenty-one strokes. In his final lap, he began counting. When he reached twenty, he made that last push, reaching out his arms as far as they would go, and . . . he touched the wall. His timing was impeccable. As he surfaced and flung off his foggy goggles, he looked to the scoreboard.

Not only did he win another gold medal, Phelps had set a new world record.

Nora Castrejon

In 2010, Nora Castrejon was a young Latina high school sophomore living in Chicago who felt stuck in a life and a community that offered little, if any, opportunities. During the school year, Nora was unmotivated in the classroom;

no matter the subject, she couldn't bring herself to care about her studies. She did the work, but she wasn't mentally engaged. Then, during the summers, she was overwhelmed by a sense of fear that was driven by her unsafe neighbourhood, which suffered from crime and poverty. At that point, Nora wasn't sure if she'd survive her teenage years; she was looking for a source of inspiration.

Late in her sophomore year, Nora learned about a program that we offer: No Barriers Learning AFAR. The program aims to ensure that all youth, no matter their background or ability, have an opportunity to experience the world and find their place within it. Nora applied to the program and even encouraged her teachers and peers to apply as well. A few weeks later, she learned that she was selected as part of a group that would travel to Costa Rica.

This was momentous. Nora had never really travelled far from home, let alone travel outside of the country. This would be a gigantic leap out of her comfort zone. This made her mother wary. However, Nora convinced her mother that such an opportunity would allow her to escape the violence that surrounded her and dodge the financial barriers that had been in her way for so long. So, that summer, Nora was off to Costa Rica.

Nora's Costa Rica trip was eye-opening and inspiring. Leading up to that trip, Nora had been withdrawn in her community and at school. However, the Learning AFAR experience encouraged her to reach beyond her comfort zone and engage with people she normally would not talk to. While in Costa Rica, she interacted with a family that quickly became close friends. Although it was unlike her to do so, she began to share fears, laughs, and tears. For the first time, she experienced the deeper meaning of fun, diversity, maturity, and unconditional friendship. And it gave her a new insight into her own Mexican American heritage.

Nora's trip to Costa Rica prepared her to live and to adjust to a different setting. Because of Learning AFAR, she emerged into a nonconformist, leader, and thinker; most importantly, she has enjoyed collaborating with people who have divergent point of views. As she says of her experience:

> No longer am I unmotivated; I'm an enthusiastic person, and I consistently strive to help those around me who are "unmotivated." This program opened many doors for me. It showed me that I could take my future into my own hands. Traveling to Costa Rica spurred a desire to not only see but to engage with the world around me; and it allowed me to see how much the world had to offer and how different people live their lives and how we were ultimately connected by the same forces.

In fall 2012, Nora was selected as a Gates Millennium Scholar, and she started her freshman year at Brown University. Only a few years earlier, she was unsure she would even finish high school. Now she was joining the elite ranks of the Ivy League—on a full-ride scholarship, no less. Nora thrived in college, even interning at the

Cook County State's Attorney's Office in the Juvenile Justice Bureau, where she saw first-hand how important it is to help at-risk youth before they enter the criminal justice system. Today, her Vision is shaped by her desire to focus on public interest law and advocate for policy to help disadvantaged communities. And because of those moments of Reach—learning how to go beyond her comfort zone—she is well on her way.

HOW YOU REACH

Now that you have seen some examples of how other people have implemented Reach in their lives, it's time for you to roll up your sleeves and get your hands dirty. When we say get your hands dirty, we mean we want you to leave your comfort zone. As Erik Weihenmayer says, "Everyone is reaching for something. The process of reaching is about getting comfortable in an environment that in its very nature is uncomfortable."

So . . .

Start with Your Vision

Running a 5K is a good goal—if you are someone who ultimately wants to become a runner and has never participated in a race before. But is such a goal relevant to your Vision? We want you to dig deep here and find out what goals will actually help you live within the words of your Vision Statement.

But remember, for us, Reach is not just about setting a goal. It's about overcoming adversity. Think about the things that are truly standing in your way for growing as a person. What makes your knees shake with fear but is also critical to your Vision?

Whatever it is you're setting out to do, make sure it's aligned with your purpose.

Draw Your Roadmap

On a sheet of blank paper, write and circle the words "You Are Here" at the top of the page, and write your Vision at the bottom. Then draw a road from your circle all the way to the Vision. Along your road, write out the series of goals that will lead you toward achieving that Vision. These are activities that will build upon each other that ultimately result in you climbing that mountain, running that division, repairing that important relationship, or whatever it is you have set out to do.

Embrace the Uncertainty

Trying something new takes you to an uncertain, possibly scary place. Questions of doubt and fear may begin to bubble up. *What if I can't do this? What if I fail? Who will judge me?* A big part of setting and achieving your Reach is accepting the struggle that is inherent in the learning process. Now is the time to embrace the challenge.

Identify a First Step

This is critical. When you look at the goals on your roadmap, you need to break them all down into the tiniest, most achievable steps. Remember that the first steps are not only intended to help move you one step closer to your vision; they are also intended to get you in the practice of trying something new every day. In short, keep it small and keep it simple.

Set a Date

In order to instil some level of accountability in this first step, set a date. Pick when you will complete this first step and put it on your calendar.

Below is a short list of examples of first steps others have taken related to their Reach.

Reach	First Step
Extend beyond my leadership role at work and become an advocate for economically disadvantaged people.	Identify people in my life who are already involved in this work and seek their counsel.
Improve my health and fitness through running.	Find a local race and run my first 5K.
Build a daily routine that prioritizes healthy living.	Review my daily schedule and build in opportunities for wellness and movement.

Reach	First Step
Bring my passion for the environment to my family.	Assess my family's current awareness and engagement in the environment and identify areas for improvement.
Challenge my assumptions about work-life balance, and find ways to better integrate the things that are most important to me.	Track where I am spending my energy day to day and determine if my time is aligned with my priorities.

Make Reach a Habit

It's important to remember that the act of Reach is not about a giant change overnight. Rather, it is achieved by carrying out a series of small steps that become habitual over time. As you get used to reaching, you'll start to think, "Hey, this isn't so bad after all."

In *The Power of Habit*, author and award-winning journalist Charles Duhigg frames habit as a neurological exercise that can be shaped by rewards. In short, all of us are driven by cravings, and if we can link those cravings to our actions, we can form habits.

Here is a look at the habit-forming system that Duhigg developed:

CUE + ROUTINE + REWARD = HABIT

Let's say your Vision is to turn your love of writing fiction into a career. You know you have potential with a pen, and you're brimming with story ideas. There's just one problem: you never actually find the time to write.

In Duhigg's system, you are going to start by creating a **Cue**. This is a trigger that will tell you it's time to engage in your desired habit. For you and your ambition to become a professional writer, this might be a notebook and pen (or a laptop) that you set on your bedside table before you go to sleep at night. Now set your alarm for an hour before you regularly would wake up. When your alarm goes off, your Cue will be there to remind you to get your butt in a chair and write.

Now comes the **Routine**. This is the activity that your Cue triggers. For sixty uninterrupted minutes, you write in your notebook or type away on your laptop, letting those ideas you've been holding in just spill out of you. (Here's a tip: to ensure your writing is uninterrupted, use an hourglass timer instead of your phone so you're not tempted to check social media and distract yourself from your writing.)

Finally, the **Reward**—this will be something that you have negotiated with yourself before even beginning this process. What's that thing you crave that would get you to sit for an hour and just write? For some, it may be food related. Others might choose a television show to watch. Whatever it is, it has to be something that will make you get out of bed rather than just hitting the snooze button.

If done right, the end result of this system is a **Habit**. You will have trained your brain to link your craving to your routine; in doing so, you will continue to engage in your new routine over and over again, whether it's writing that novel one hour at a time, running each morning, or rehearsing that song you want to sing.

There is nobody who understands Routine, Reward, and Reach better than Mandy Harvey. So, let's go back to where we left her at the beginning of this chapter.

MANDY'S GOLDEN BUZZER MOMENT

In Mandy Harvey's story, we saw that she had several Reach moments that helped move her closer to her Vision. She had an important Reach when she sat down with her father to record a song for the first time since losing her hearing. When Mandy decided to brave the stage at Jay's Bistro and perform for the first time again at that open mic night, that was a key Reach moment for her. As was the Reach when she recorded her first album of cover songs. All of these milestones showcase Mandy's courage and her willingness to try even when the odds were against her. But for Mandy, she believes her most critical *Reach* moment came when she was first asked to write an original song.

A few years after she lost her hearing, Mandy lost a friend within her community named Kelsey. Kelsey's parents asked Mandy if she would write a song to be sung at Kelsey's memorial service. Mandy agreed, and she wrote her first song, one that she titled, "Going Home."

Through the process of writing the song and then singing it at Kelsey's memorial, Mandy realized what had been missing in her journey—that feeling of thinking beyond herself. That first song wasn't for her; it was for Kelsey and Kelsey's parents. That's what made it so meaningful. When Mandy had lost the last of her hearing, she had experienced a small death. When she wrote that song for Kelsey's memory and shared her gift with Kelsey's family and friends, that feeling of being able to give a piece of herself to others, that felt like a rebirth.

Prompted by that Reach moment, Mandy began penning more original songs. When writing lyrics, she chose subjects that were personal, weaving together stories and emotions from the fabric of her own life. When she had enough songs, she recorded her first original album, *All of Me.*

The album led to Mandy touring around the country and playing for new audiences outside of Jay's Bistro— with most audiences unaware Mandy was deaf. Now that she was backed by a full band, Mandy had perfected her methodology for how to pick up on cues and ensure that she was in tune. She would start each show with a tuning app on her phone, finding that middle C. She would go barefoot, her feet touching the floor of the stage so that the vibrations from the other instruments could travel through her body. And she would keep in constant communication with her band members. As she has said, "Playing with a band is all about communication. We are paying attention to each other. Lots of visual contact, as well, all the songs are well rehearsed and if there are any differences, we can sign to each other and get information fast."

At one of Mandy's shows, unbeknownst to her, a television producer was sitting in the audience listening to Mandy sing. That producer worked on *America's Got Talent*, a competition show that invites undiscovered talent to perform on national television. The producer was so impressed with Mandy that they invited her to audition for the judges of *America's Got Talent*. Mandy, who had never seen the show before, agreed to it.

The day Mandy showed up to her audition, she remembers there was a problem with the Golden Buzzer—a button that the judges can press if a performance is so good that they just want to send the participant straight through to the live show at the end of the season. One of the techs told the producers that the Golden Buzzer was broken. Simon Cowell, the famously hard-to-impress creator of the show, said that it wouldn't matter since it was too early in the season to use the buzzer anyway.

Eventually, they did fix that buzzer, and Mandy went on stage to sing. Standing there shoeless on the stage, wearing a red dress and playing her ukulele, Mandy sang one of her original songs, "Try." She performed the song in a way that was smooth and steady, almost subdued. Watching her on that stage, one might have gotten the sense that Mandy didn't feel the need to show off her vocal range; instead, she would rather have an intimate conversation with the audience. And that conversation had the audience on their feet halfway through the song, their hearts and eyes clearly filled with emotion. When Mandy finished singing, Simon Cowell let the tension hang in the air of the studio for only a moment before saying, "Mandy, I don't think you're going to need a translator for this" and then he pressed that Golden Buzzer. As the audience cheered wildly and confetti fluttered around Mandy, tears of joy streamed down her face. (If you have never seen Mandy's audition on *AGT*, put this book down immediately and watch her performance on YouTube. Also, make sure you have tissues handy.)

When Mandy's Golden Buzzer moment aired two months later, the video of her singing on *AGT* went mega-viral. At last check, the video has been viewed more than 500 million times. And so, once again, Mandy's life changed. She was suddenly being interviewed by *Rolling Stone*, *Time*, and *Billboard*. She was asked to sing in venues she had only dreamed of playing, like The Iridium in New York City. And she was invited to tell her story on nationally televised morning shows like the *Today* show.

But of all the things that grew out of that performance on *America's Got Talent*, the greatest reward for Mandy was the conversation that she had inspired. People everywhere were seeing Mandy's journey and suddenly talking about overcoming adversity in their own lives. Mandy didn't go on *AGT* hoping she would become famous. Instead, she wanted people to see that she hadn't let her disability hold her back. In fact, she had found a way to add to her identity, not take away from it. As she has often said, "Even minus my hearing, I'm a more complete person."

Every one of us will have unique Reach moments. Moreover, we won't have just one Reach moment, but many. While Mandy pinpoints that first song she wrote for Kelsey as her primary Reach moment, she has had several smaller Reach moments along her journey, each one forcing her to have the courage to try something that might be uncomfortable or challenging.

It's also important to remember that Mandy didn't set her sights on *America's Got Talent* the day she lost her hearing. She didn't aim to be a spokesperson for the deaf community. Her steps or Reaches were much smaller, more concrete. And that's an important lesson for all of us. Many of us are inclined to set big and general objectives like "I'm going to get fit" or "I'm going to give up drinking." What we know from research is that big lofty goals need to be broken down into small bite-size chunks: "I'm going to go sing with my dad" or "I'll sing one song at Jay's Bistro." Without the small day-by-day, week-by-week Reaches, most of us give up the pursuit of the lofty goal. As we mentioned earlier, it's why over eighty per cent of all New Year's pledges are never fulfilled. Make sure you keep this bite-size approach in mind as you continue to practice Reach.

CHAPTER THREE

Alchemy

"It's not what happens to you,
but how you react to it that matters."
—*Epictetus*

TURNING PAIN INTO PURPOSE

Before Jose Rene "J.R." Martinez learned to crawl, his father had already walked out on him and his mother, Maria, an immigrant who had fled the political turmoil and violence of El Salvador in the 1980s in search of a better life in America. As a young boy growing up in Louisiana—and then Arkansas—J.R. watched his mother work tirelessly to bring home a pay cheque that would allow her to both put food on their table and send money back to her young daughters who were still in El Salvador with family. J.R.'s mother scrubbed toilets, she nannied, she worked the graveyard shift at a food distribution plant; all the while, J.R. was a latchkey kid forced to shoulder the responsibilities that his father had shirked. So long before J.R. Martinez reached the age of adulthood, he had left his childhood far behind.

This explains a lot about why, even as a teenager, he was so mature and forward-thinking when it came to making life decisions. When J.R. was finishing up his junior year of high school, he looked around his tough Arkansas town with its gangs and its drugs, and he realized that if he stayed there, he would be led down the wrong path. But if he could get out before it was too late, J.R. might have a chance at a better life.

So, after J.R. and his mother visited one of Maria's friends in Dalton, Georgia—a town with less crime and more opportunity—J.R. tried to convince his mother to relocate there. Maria was reluctant: she had worked her way up to a supervisor position at the distribution centre, and she was finally earning good, reliable money. But J.R. was determined, so he made a deal with his mother: he would travel out to Dalton and stay with his mother's friend for a few weeks during the summer between his junior and senior years of high school; and if he could find a job and an apartment for them, Maria would join him. Maria took her son's bet, and J.R. caught the next Greyhound bus to Georgia. He promptly secured a job as a forklift driver at a carpet factory and then found an apartment. That would be the last time J.R.'s mother would underestimate his determination.

In Dalton, J.R. established a good life for himself and his mother. With his easy smile and his curly-haired charisma, he found friends (and girlfriends) without a problem. While he wasn't the star player on the high school football team, he was one of the most integral and spirited members. As J.R. will tell you, he had solid skills, but you wouldn't find him on the highlight reel. Instead, if the camera panned to the sidelines, you'd often see him there in his #36 jersey rooting on his teammates louder than anyone else. It was during that time when J.R. discovered that lifting up others was actually a source of energy for him. And whether he was on the field or off, J.R. was cheering on his friends and fellow players.

After J.R. graduated from high school, he found himself at a crossroads. He knew he didn't want to keep working in the factory for the rest of his life; but, at least for now, college didn't feel like the right option either. Then, one day, J.R. walked past an advertisement for the US Army, and six words suddenly changed his entire life:

Be. All. That. You. Can. Be.

On September 11, 2002—exactly one year after the Twin Towers fell in the 9/11 attack on America—J.R. met with an army recruiter and boarded a bus that would take him to the Armed Services Recruiting Center in Tennessee. Suddenly, J.R.'s life was filled with purpose . . . and steely-eyed drill instructors and endless push-ups and gruelling runs. (For some reason, the hardest concept for J.R. to get used to in the army was military time. His commanding officer made a habit of barking, "Martinez, what time is it?" and J.R. consistently responded with the incorrect time, unable to do the conversion quickly enough. Finally, J.R. got smart and bought a watch that told military time, and he never took it off his wrist.)

In 2003, at the start of the US invasion of Iraq, J.R. received his first deployment orders. He was heading to the Middle East. Along with the rest of the 2nd Brigade of the 502nd Infantry Regiment, J.R. boarded an airliner that took him to a staging area in Kuwait and then onto the war zone in Iraq. J.R. was one of nearly 150,000 US troops deployed to that region. Tragically, he would also be one of an untold number of soldiers who would see their lives changed by combat forever.

It happened while J.R. was behind the wheel of a Humvee as he led a convoy into Karbala, a city in Central Iraq. J.R. had been in combat for only a month. As he steered the vehicle toward the dusty city, his front left tire hit a roadside land mine, and BOOM! J.R. was suddenly caught in a spin cycle as the Humvee was flipped through the air by the explosion. Within moments, the inside of his vehicle was swallowed by fire. As J.R. details in his memoir *Full of Heart*, "The heat from the explosion roared into a fire that sounded oddly like falling rain . . . I watched as the flames licked up from the floor and my hands started to burn, the skin melting away." For J.R., in that moment, he was convinced that each heartbeat would be his last. He was going to die right there in the flames.

But thanks to several other soldiers in his unit, J.R. was pulled from the incinerating Humvee and rushed to a Black Hawk helicopter, which flew him to a local combat support hospital. Once the medics were able to ensure he was stabilized, J.R. was then medevaced to Landstuhl Regional Medical Center in Germany and, from there, transferred back to the United States.

For several weeks, J.R. was in and out of consciousness at the Brooke Army Medical Center at Fort Sam Houston in San Antonio, Texas, where his mother remained at his bedside praying for her son's survival. In that time, the doctors were treating the third-degree burns that covered thirty-four per cent of J.R.'s body, including his torso, his hands and arms, and his face. (Of note: one of the spots on his arms that was spared from the flames was the very place he wore the watch that told military time.) But it wasn't the burns that presented the most urgent concern for the medical team; rather, it was the toxic particles he had inhaled during the blast, which were threatening to fatally damage J.R.'s lungs. The doctors spent a majority of their time ventilating J.R. in hopes of clearing out his airways. Finally, after a few weeks of touch-and-go, J.R. turned a corner and he began breathing on his own.

A little over three weeks after arriving at the hospital, J.R. asked his nurse if he could see his face, which he had not yet seen. The nurse nodded and helped J.R. into a chair. For a few moments, as the nurse held the mirror, J.R. just looked down, preparing himself for what he was about to encounter. He had no idea what to expect. Finally, J.R. slowly picked his head up and his eyes met the mirror . . . and he didn't recognize the man looking back at him. All he could think was that he looked like Freddy Krueger, the hideously scarred villain from *A Nightmare on Elm Street*.

As J.R. remembers that moment, "For nineteen years of my life, I had developed a relationship with a certain identity, and suddenly that identity was taken away from me. There was someone new in that reflection of mine, and I didn't know that person. He was a stranger to me."

Gone was his megawatt smile and his curly hair. And what had replaced those things were anger and depression. To him, life would only be difficult from here on out. While the blast didn't take his legs from him, they were badly wounded and he needed assistance walking. Moreover, his hands were so severely burned that they were claw like and barely functional, which meant he would likely need his mother or an assistant always around to help him accomplish even the most basic tasks. Yes, thanks to a team of doctors, J.R. was going to live, but he couldn't imagine in that moment what he was going to live *for*.

The doctors in the burn unit informed J.R. that he would have to undergo countless surgeries over the course of many months, if not years, in order to repair the damage done to his body in the blast. He had a long way to go before he *might* be able to recognize himself again in the mirror. As J.R. started on that long road to recovery, there was one question that never left his mind: *Why did this happen to me?*

One answer to that question came after J.R. had been in the hospital for several months. With the help of surgeries and rehab, J.R. had managed to get himself moved out of the ICU to a step-down unit where he was able to at least talk to staff during the night shift. For J.R., a guy who had always had such an outgoing personality, the ICU was confining; now he could be chatting up the nurses. Then, when he moved to convalescent housing on base, he had even more freedom to move about and socialize. Almost immediately, he noticed a shift in his own outlook on life as he engaged more with other people. And, before long, the staff noticed this shift in J.R., too, and they thought his outgoing personality could be beneficial to the other patients.

One day, about six months after he had arrived at Fort Sam Houston, a nurse approached J.R. and asked him if he would consider speaking to another burn victim who was new to the floor and struggling with the reality of his new life. J.R. was reluctant—*what could he say to comfort another patient?*—but he agreed. As J.R. entered the hospital room, he noticed the lights were off and the curtains were closed even though the patient was awake and it was almost noon. As J.R. started to speak, he realized that the young man just needed someone to fill the silence.

So that's what J.R. did. He talked about his own experiences and his adversities, and he made sure that the other patient could really see J.R.'s burns and scars. In doing so, J.R. wanted to help the patient realize that J.R. could empathize—that he wasn't alone on this difficult journey. As J.R. was leaving the room that day, a light appeared behind him. As he looked back into the room, he saw that the young man was opening up the curtains, finally letting in the outside world. The significance of that moment was not lost on J.R.

Before long, J.R. was visiting more and more patients in the burn unit, encouraging them and rooting for them much in the same way he did back on the football team in high school. He started making his "rounds," as he called them—going from room to room and visiting with patients in the mornings before attending his own physical therapy sessions in the afternoons. And just like his days with the football team, J.R. found that lifting up others was still a source of energy for him.

DEFINING ALCHEMY

Alchemy is the process of turning challenges into opportunities to grow. When we face intense adversity in our lives, we have a tendency to become deflated or allow negativity to fester; this only hamstrings our efforts to overcome that adversity. For us, this Life Element, which is arguably one of the more difficult concepts to understand, is about how you *think* about the challenges in your life. It's about cultivating a spirit of optimism and positivity despite the adversities that we must confront. At its core, Alchemy is a *mindset*.

Why the word "Alchemy?" The origin of the word and its concepts date back to the Middle Ages (and even earlier) when alchemists believed in the potential of turning one natural substance into another—gold being the most sought-after prize. These alchemists, who were essentially precursors to modern chemists, were studying the art of transmuting base metals into gold. Robert Boyle and Sir Isaac Newton, the founding fathers of chemistry and physics, respectively, were serious students of alchemy. And while the alchemical process would ultimately prove impossible and later dismissed as mysticism, its practitioners did help inspire many of the techniques and procedures adopted by modern laboratories around the globe. Often through happy accidents, several alchemists would uncover other scientific advancements in medicine and chemistry that we still use today.

We like the word "Alchemy" because it conveys the sense that unbelievable transformation is possible even if improbable. In fact, one definition of Alchemy is that it's *a seemingly magical process of transformation, creation, or combination.* And that neatly describes the ambition of this Life Element, which is to help you find ways to transform challenges into opportunities, even when such a transformation seems impossible to you.

In our research, we found it fascinating that throughout history, people have tried to come up with creative ways to express this complicated concept through language, symbols, and proverbial phrases. We have all heard, "When life gives you lemons, make lemonade," or "When life hands you olives, make olive oil." Another symbol of this concept is the centuries-old Japanese art form of *kintsugi*, or "golden repair." When a ceramic bowl falls and breaks into many pieces, *kintsugi* is the art of putting the broken pottery pieces together not with glue but with gold. *Kintsugi* teaches us that there is beauty and value in our scars and encourages us to approach them in a positive way. *Kintsugi* instructs us that instead of feeling ashamed and hiding our struggles, cracks, and brokenness, we should embrace them, highlight them, and celebrate our growth from them. Even our scars can be transformed into "gold."

Indeed, the ability to look at some of our most difficult struggles through a lens of optimism and positivity is not easy. But as we mentioned above, Alchemy is a *mindset*. And this is different than a *skillset*. If your skillset is what you know how to do—ride a bike, scuba dive, track leopards, and so forth—then your mindset is the attitude you have while doing it. Do you see the distinction?

Mindset underlies everything else you do in life, and it is certainly critical to every step you take on this No Barriers' journey. When you become an Alchemist, you realize that your old way of thinking about something no longer fits. You've broken your own mould and crafted a new worldview. It's a view that believes in every adversity lies a tremendous opportunity.

Consider J.R. Martinez's journey in the framework of Alchemy. For most people, if they experienced a trauma like his, they would find it difficult to get out of bed and face the day, let alone put themselves out there to be a source of inspiration the way that J.R. did. But J.R. managed to shift his mindset and see an opportunity in his adversity. With J.R., he clearly seems naturally inclined toward optimism, but not all of us are wired that way. As J.R. says, "Yes, I'm a positive guy, but I'm human, too." He acknowledges that he has his moments of doubt and vulnerability (as we will see more about later in this chapter). The same could be said of Erik and Mandy, two other stories we have explored in depth so far. In order to overcome their adversities, they didn't have to be superhuman; they just needed to shift their mindsets and choose to respond to their circumstances in positive ways.

And that's another key principle of Alchemy: *choice*. We must always remember that we have a choice in how we respond to the difficulties we face. As Viktor Frankl says, *"Between stimulus and response there is a space. In that space is our power to choose our response. In our response lies our growth and our freedom."* So, the gap that happens between when a challenge happens and the outcome, that is when you have a choice. And the outcome will be determined by your choice.

WHY ALCHEMY MATTERS

For starters, your mindset matters to your happiness, and it can be a key driver for better health. We have had thousands of people who go through the No Barriers program and then credit the program with dramatically improving their lives both with respect to their happiness and their physical well-being. The essence of Alchemy is to tap into your ability to truly believe that *what's within you is stronger than what's in your way*; ninety per cent of our participants self-report this to be true after our programs.

Meanwhile, nearly eighty per cent say they "understand what it means to harness adversity" and agree that they can start to "face [their] challenges with a positive attitude." Simply knowing that you have a choice engenders within you a sense of liberation and independence that will have a real effect on your attitude.

In Erik Weihenmayer's book, *Adversity Advantage*, he makes the point that when tackling big challenges, mindset trumps skillset every time. In this chapter, you'll learn the tools that we use in our programs to train your brain to look at each adversity as an opportunity and to approach it with optimism, hope, and positivity.

To underscore this notion that Alchemy (i.e., mindset) can have a profound impact on your happiness and health, here are the words of Shawn Achor, author of *The Happiness Advantage*: "When we are positive, our brains become more engaged, creative, motivated, energetic, resilient, and productive. This discovery has been repeatedly supported by research in psychology and neuroscience, management studies, and the bottom lines of organizations around the world." The benefits that accrue from positivity are many, and they will be tremendously helpful in your efforts to overcome adversity in your life.

Your mindset also matters to your success. With today's ever-changing global marketplace, scientists suggest that the half-life of a learned skill is now approaching three years. Think about that for a moment. Your contract with your cell phone service provider could last longer than the marketability of the skills you are learning today. That means *change* is the new norm. The skills we learn today will not be the skills we need in a few years to be successful. Employers are increasingly looking for employees with the right mindset, realizing that everyone will have to learn new skills as they go.

The right mindset can, of course, mean many things, but a key idea is how employees think about and approach the challenges they face. Do they look at them as opportunities, or do they give up in the face of adversity? As Barbara Fredrickson (author of *Positivity*) found in a meta-analysis of over 300 research studies, "Positivity produces success in life as much as it reflects success in life. Regardless of whether success was measured as a satisfying marriage, a larger salary, or better health, positivity mattered."

So now that you have a clearer understanding of what Alchemy is and what role it plays in your journey here, let's hear from some of our Grand Philosophers in order to take a deeper dive into the foundations of Alchemy.

Grand Philosopher #1
Epictetus

Epictetus was a Greco-Roman philosopher who became one of the most prominent voices in *Stoicism*, a school of philosophy that highlights the significance of distinguishing between what is in our control versus what is not in our control.

An influential thinker of his time and even today, Epictetus had a life story that clearly shaped the way he viewed the world. Nearly two thousand years ago, Epictetus was born a slave, forced to serve a master even though he suffered from a badly crippled leg. Yet, enslaved and disabled, Epictetus still managed to develop an affirming way of looking at the world, one that stressed choice rather than circumstance. As he explains:

> Sickness is a hindrance to the body, but not to your ability to choose, unless that is your choice. Lameness is a hindrance to the leg, but not to your ability to choose. Say this to yourself with regard to everything that happens, then you will see such obstacles as hindrances to something else, but not to yourself.

You can hear the echoes of Viktor Frankl in Epictetus's words, right? Just as Frankl refused to let his imprisonment by the Nazis strip him of his ability to choose how he met the world each day, Epictetus did not allow his circumstances as a crippled slave to take away his freedom to choose his mindset. In both cases, choice and mindset are at the heart of each of these men's existence, and they are what aided Frankl and Epictetus in pushing through challenging situations.

After decades of enslavement, Epictetus was finally freed, and he spent the remainder of his years studying and teaching philosophy in Rome and parts of Greece. His public speeches, which were later preserved by his students, had an empowering message that forced his audience to differentiate between those things that were in their control and those things that were not. For Epictetus, things that are in your control are desire, opinion, aversion, and the actions you take, whereas the things you do not have power over are such things as your health, property, and other people's actions.

Once you can determine where in your life you have the ability to choose and where you do not, you will find it easier to frame your own mindset. This is the key to Alchemy. As Epictetus lays out succinctly, this should be your objective: "To make the best of what is in our power, and take the rest as it occurs."

Grand Philosopher #2
Martin Seligman

For the better part of the twentieth century, the fields of psychology and psychiatry spent much of their energy exploring what made depressed people depressed. But in the late 1990s, some psychologists and psychiatrists started to approach their studies from a new angle: *What makes happy people happy?*

Martin Seligman, a professor and noted pioneer of the positive psychology movement, was one such person who decided that he wanted to focus on the strengths and potential of humans rather than the pathologies and disorders. For Seligman, it's not just about finding out what's wrong with you; it's equally (if not more) important to find out what's right with you.

Now, as we've discussed in earlier chapters, the word "happiness" can be tricky. It means different things to different people. When Seligman talks about studying what makes happy people happy, he's not referring to a sense of exuberance or glee (words a thesaurus might offer); instead, he's using the term in a way that is akin to how we talk about happiness at No Barriers: it's about that genuinely satisfying feeling that comes from discovering value within yourself.

Within the context of Alchemy, Seligman's most applicable ideas come in his studies on *optimism* versus *pessimism*. According to Seligman, he has been studying the two opposing worldviews for a quarter century, and he has crafted discrete understandings of each.

As Seligman relays in his book *Learned Optimism*:

The defining characteristic of pessimists is that they tend to believe bad events will last a long time, will undermine everything they do, and are their own fault. The optimists, who are confronted with the same hard knocks of this world, think about misfortune in the opposite way. They tend to believe defeat is just a temporary setback, that its causes are confined to this one case. The optimists believe defeat is not their fault—circumstances, bad luck, or other people brought it about. Such people are unfazed by defeat. Confronted by a bad situation, they perceive it as a challenge and try harder.

For most of us, we interpret these two personality types—optimists and pessimists—in fairly generic and broad terms. An optimist has a sunny outlook on life, while the pessimist sees the world through a rainy lens, right? Or how about these well-worn expressions: glass half full or glass half empty.

What is so instructive about Seligman's explanation is his more nuanced characterizations. In the above passage, Seligman is going a step further and exploring how each personality type internalizes events. While a challenging experience is objectively the same for the pessimist and the optimist, the pessimist is more likely to give up, while the optimist will try again. And since success often comes only after several failed attempts, who is more likely to succeed—the optimist who is unfazed by failure or the pessimist whose mindset blocks them from trying again and again?

Now, interestingly, Seligman goes on to note in his book that oftentimes, pessimists are more accurate in their view of reality:

Depressed people—most of whom turn out to be pessimists—accurately judge how much control they have. Nondepressed people—optimists, for the most part—believe they have much more control over things than they actually do, particularly when they are helpless and have no control at all. Overall, then, there is clear evidence that nondepressed people distort reality in a self-serving direction and depressed people tend to see reality accurately.

Boiling that down, a pessimist's view of events more closely adheres to reality, while the optimist is, in some ways, deluding themselves, even if only a little.

And this begs the question: with Alchemy, are we just asking you to pretend everything is rosy? In some ways, the answer is yes. But having that optimistic mindset even in the face of a grim reality is critical for you to push through seemingly impossible obstacles. Optimism gives you the energy to overcome challenges.

With those foundational ideas in mind, let's take a look at how others have put Alchemy to work in the service of turning challenges into opportunities to grow.

ALCHEMY IN PRACTICE
Kate Leyden Merrill

In late 2019, Kate Leyden Merrill secluded herself in a hotel for two days to have the time and space she needed to focus on a revamped strategic plan for her bakery, Edge of Sweetness, a beloved establishment in the Edgewater neighbourhood in Chicago. After her business partner left and Kate dedicated more focus to her business strategy, the married mother of three was confident that 2020 was going to be the breakout year for the bakery. While Kate loved the act of baking—something she had been doing since she was twelve—her greatest reward was in seeing first-hand the reactions to her cookies. At the very beginning of her strategic plan, she wrote:

> Vision: In every interaction with Edge of Sweetness our customers will experience our integrity, our community and the comforts of home. Every person will feel our personal touch.

Years before, Kate had encountered a man who confided that he had nearly killed himself earlier that day. He shared that he hadn't gone through with it because a stranger he passed on the sidewalk had smiled and asked him how he was doing. It is a story Kate has never forgotten, and it's what inspired her to include the imperative about every person feeling the personal touch in her vision statement.

The bakery got off to a strong start in 2020, hitting its sales targets the first two months. But by early March, with the impending spread of COVID-19 across the United States, like many other retail shop owners across the country, Kate began making preparations to shift her plans. Her first thought was how to keep the customers and the employees healthy while they were at the bakery.

She retrained all employees on the health protocols in the store and ensured that everyone was taking the necessary precautions. But as March wore on, she was faced with a bigger question: should she keep the bakery open or temporarily shut it down? She brought her staff together and asked employees for their input. After a long discussion about the facts and the concerns, her team was in full agreement that they would support Kate whatever she decided. Ultimately, she made the decision to close temporarily.

After all the progress she made for her business in the first few months of the year, the COVID-19 crisis felt like a gut punch. It was a bit of a flashback to her days as a collegiate runner when she had suffered bursitis in her hip. Despite having her season derailed, she optimistically told herself then that this challenge was a learning experience which would somehow help her later in life. Flash forward to 2020, Kate thought maybe now was that time. Again, she embraced her struggle and pivoted her bakery's business model to meet the new challenges by creating a "Weekly Stock-Up Sale" for her loyal customers. She applied and received her Paycheck Protection Program loan. And she reconnected with one of her former colleagues.

For twenty-two years, Kate had served as a trauma nurse at a hospital on the west side of Chicago. She had thrived on being able to help and support patients who were the sickest of the sick. When she spoke with her former colleague, a dear friend, she told her that she feared the hospital was heading for an overwhelming surge in patients. With her community facing its greatest health crisis in a generation, Kate felt she needed to pivot once again. She felt she needed to answer the call from the governor for nurse support. Although this decision came with sizable risks for her—exposing her to numerous patients with COVID-19 and limiting her ability to focus on the bakery—Kate knew this is what she needed to do for her friends at the hospital and for the patients she could help.

She then asked her husband, a carpenter, what he thought about the idea. He said, "If you do this, I would worry about you every day. That said, if my parent or our child caught this disease, I would want you there to help." With his full support, she posted a message to Facebook explaining that she was wanting to serve as a licensed and registered trauma nurse "to help our patients get through this troubling time in the best way I can."

It did not take long before Kate was offered to be a short-term nurse at the hospital where she had previously worked. The hospital had numerous COVID-19 cases. She described her floor and the number of suffering patients all around her as a "war zone." But perhaps the cruellest aspect of this pandemic, Kate said, is the way that it disconnects people from each other. Patients are disconnected from their families and aren't able to be with them in the hospital. Because of all of the protective gear, nurses' interactions with patients can feel very impersonal.

In order to adequately protect herself in the hospital, Kate again had to adapt. She adopted the standard safety protocol—wearing a face shield, respirator mask, a gown, and gloves—that create both physical and emotional barriers between her and her patients. But in order to stay true to her mission to care for her patients with a personal touch, she always made a point to talk to the patient, stroke their head, pat their shoulder, and touch their hands whenever she's in the room with them.

The COVID-19 pandemic delivered a devastating blow to small businesses and frontline healthcare workers. While many would give up in the face of her obstacles, time after time Kate chose to pivot toward positivity and connection in the midst of these unprecedented challenges. After Kate completed her work at the hospital, she again embraced her inner alchemist and immediately started laying the foundation for the triumphant return of the bakery.

Billy Lister

What if each day you woke up only to discover that you could no longer do something you could do just the day before? One day, you find yourself having trouble typing on a keyboard—something you've always been able to do. The next day, you can't tie your shoes. The next, you can't button your shirt. This continues until you no longer have mobility and function on much of the left side of your body . . . and you have no idea why this is happening.

This is what Billy Lister experienced when he was just seventeen years old. For four weeks, Billy slowly lost the functions of his left-hand side. What he would later learn was that he was essentially having a stroke in slow motion. One year earlier, he had undergone surgery for a birth defect that left him with an extra set of blood vessels in the brain. Although the surgery was a success and had saved his life, it had an unintended and undetected side effect: swelling in his brain. That swelling is what led to Billy's stroke. And the stroke left Billy disabled.

Until that stroke, Billy had been an active teenager, and he had dreamed of being a professional athlete. He played everything from soccer to basketball, baseball, football, and lacrosse. After the stroke, he had to stop playing sports altogether. His new reality was devastating. So instead of confronting it, he simply denied it. Billy got stuck in the wrong mindset, and what he needed was Alchemy.

For the better part of twelve years following that, he was in a permanent state of denial, and this state manifested itself in vices and addiction. Billy turned to alcohol and drugs to dull the pain. For him, it came down to the fact that he did not want the body he was living in, so he was destroying it every single day.

This denial was cast into high relief for Billy one day in his mid-twenties when he was living in New York and working on Wall Street. This particular day, he was exiting the subway with some friends when one of them asked Billy why he was limping. Billy responded, "There's nothing wrong with me." In that moment, Billy realized that he had convinced himself that he was the same kid as he was before the stroke. He was living in this negative fantasy world. He was sustaining his life, but he wasn't living it. For Billy, that was when he hit his low point.

Then, in 2009, Billy decided to take a risk and attend a No Barriers Summit, which he had heard about through a friend. Even signing up for the summit was outside of his comfort zone. By doing so, he was acknowledging that he needed a change, and that's never easy. But the risk was worth the reward.

As Billy recounts about his experience at the summit:

I found a light inside of me that started to shine again. I found a family from across the nation who inspired, supported, and challenged me—they still do. I found hope. I didn't yet know what would come of it, but I knew I was changed. It was like I was standing all alone in a completely pitch-black room and No Barriers tapped me on the shoulder and said, "Billy, the light switch is right behind you."

Two years later, Billy was invited to a para-triathlon in San Diego through Challenge Athletes Foundation, a group he had met at the No Barriers Summit. It was at that event that Billy got on a bicycle for the first time in fourteen years. His balance was terrible, and he didn't know how to use his body. The truth was, he hadn't tested his level of function in years. But in that first attempt, he found a new passion. If the summit had transformed him mentally, that para-triathlon transformed him physically. He wanted to ride again.

In 2013, he moved from New York to Orange County, California, and dedicated himself to training. Shortly thereafter, he got invited to a Paralympics race. He showed up to the starting line, and he raced well. Suddenly, he was hooked, and he's been a racer ever since.

As Billy says, "In just a few short years, I went on to fully dedicate myself to the realm of Paralympic cycling. In 2016, at the Team USA Paralympic Trials, I finished as the first overall male two-wheel cyclist, automatically qualifying my spot for the Rio de Janeiro Paralympic Games—the culmination of years of blind determination, all of which was spawned by the No Barriers Mindset."

Today, Billy's dedication to his sport is apparent in his daily routine. Being a professional athlete now, he'll have anywhere from one to four workouts. His strength and conditioning lasts two to two and a half hours, and then he hops on his bike and will ride for two to four hours. He'll repeat this several times a day. But his training is more than just physical. He does mindfulness work in order to train his brain to be in a certain state of discomfort every single day. All of this work for Billy will hopefully pay off in the next Paralympics, where he pledges to compete.

Here are Billy's own words on his Alchemist mindset: "Just say yes. Yes to everything. When you're in those dark moments of your life, those doldrums, those valleys, it's so easy to say no and to take the already beaten path . . . But saying yes, that's the hard part and it just gets easier after that."

BECOMING AN ALCHEMIST

So now it's your turn.

The first thing you want to keep at the top of your mind as you go through the following steps is that developing an Alchemist's mindset requires effort. It's not something we're all born with. On the contrary, it seems we're more wired to hold on to negativity than positivity.

The other thing you want to remember is that Alchemy is a muscle. And as J.R. Martinez says, we all need to exercise our Alchemy muscle routinely. In fact, J.R. suggests this daily meditation as a way to start your day: "I'm going to be positive. I'm going to be in control. I'm going to be patient. I'm going to have faith. I'm going to believe." Try saying that out loud for a moment and let the words take hold.

Now let's learn how to exercise that muscle.

(1) Understanding the Art of Reframing
   a. *Take a step back.* Try to get at the 30,000-foot perspective of the situation. Are there assumptions you're making or deeply held beliefs that might be preventing you from looking at the challenge from a different perspective?
   b. *Look at where you want to go.* Stay at the 30,000-foot perspective, and remember your Vision. Where are the roadblocks from this higher-level view? Are they the same at ground-level view?

c. *Identify your choices.* Move to a different vantage point and look at the challenge from a variety of different perspectives. Could the challenge be seen as an opportunity? Could the weakness be a strength? Could the perceived unkindness simply be a lack of understanding?

d. *Choose how you want to respond.* Remember Viktor Frankl's words? "Between stimulus and response there is a space. In that space is our power to choose our response. In our response lies our growth and our freedom."

e. *Laugh a little and step into the new frame.* Never underestimate the power of humour to help you move through a challenge into a more positive outlook.

(2) Stopping the Cycle of Rumination

As Zen master Thich Nhat Hanh says, "We ruminate on suffering, regret, and sorrow. We chew on them, swallow them, bring them back up, and eat them again and again. If we're feeding our suffering while we're walking, working, eating, or talking, we are making ourselves victims of the ghosts of the past, of the future, or our worries in the present. We're not living our lives." Part of becoming an Alchemist requires you to stop dwelling on the negative.

You can stop the cycle of rumination in many ways. You can simply get moving and start doing something else. (Think exercise, watch a movie, go volunteer, etc.) Basically, you can stop the cycle by occupying your mind with something else that requires your complete attention.

If you prefer a more cognitive route to ending the cycle of rumination, you can adopt some principles that come out of the Penn Resiliency Program, a depression-prevention effort rooted in cognitive behavioural therapy that teaches nonnegative thinking:

Start with a set of Post-it notes or index cards and write one of your typical negative thoughts: things like, "Damn, not again, I suck!" or "How will I ever get a new client?" or "Why didn't they like my ideas? Don't they get it?" What's important here is to write down negative thoughts that are realistic and truly yours. Capture your inner critic, that voice in your head that's sceptical of you, of others, and of everything around you—the voice of ill will.

Once you have written out your set of usual suspects, shuffle the cards and pick one at random. Read it out loud. Then, as fast and as thoroughly as you can, dispute it! Do it out loud and with some conviction.

(3) Practicing Mindfulness
You know that feeling when you're facing a challenge and a sense of doubt paralyzes you, preventing you from pushing forward? Mindfulness helps you to keep moving through

your challenges rather than letting your challenges stop you in your tracks. Practicing mindfulness is about bringing your attention inside your body and learning to observe your circumstance from an unattached perspective.

To do this, you find a comfortable, quiet place, and you take the time to notice the sensations of your breath or thoughts coming and going in your mind. By guiding your attention in this specific way, you can be aware of your experience without imposing judgment on it. As you breathe out, you're letting go of the negative noise that troubles you. In a sense, you're taking out your internal garbage. And as you breathe in, you're imagining yourself taking in the positivity that your mindset requires.

(4) Focusing on What You Can Control

There's an energy in adversity that can be used as a fuel to propel you rather than hold you back. How you respond to that force is what determines your happiness, fulfilment, success, and so on. Your response is your Alchemy. At some point, you start to learn to focus on what you can control, and that's your response to the situation. You stop worrying about all the things you cannot control—the results of your next round of chemo, the response of an upset spouse, and so forth—and you focus on owning those things you can control.

(5) Realizing You Will Slip Up

Remember, we all have streaks of pessimism within us. But you can start to recognize the negativity that your brain often goes to more quickly to head it off. One No Barriers participant calls this "hearing the train coming before it becomes a train wreck." Once you get used to the crazy ways your brain operates, you can start to exert power and influence over your own story. Recognizing what's coming (in your own brain) is half the battle toward heading it off.

Now that you have learned the foundations of Alchemy and what it means to become an Alchemist, let's check back in on J.R. Martinez's journey.

THE ART OF THE POSSIBLE

Word of J.R.'s visits with patients floated around the Brooke Army Medical Center and into the office of Norma Guerra, the chief of public affairs. Norma saw an opportunity for J.R. to be a spokesman for the burn survivor community, and she began sending him out on interviews. He spoke at luncheons on base, he spoke to local news reporters, he spoke at nonprofit fundraisers for wounded veterans. And each time he spoke, J.R. managed to create more and more opportunities to build awareness for burn survivors. Local access TV interviews in San Antonio turned into nationally syndicated shows inviting him to speak about his trauma.

CBS's *60 Minutes* sat down with J.R. to hear his story. Even Oprah interviewed J.R. for her show.

And so, on the surface, it appeared everything was going smoothly for J.R. and his recovery. But while J.R. was able to effectively present an image of confidence to his doctors at the hospital, to reporters in television interviews, and to audiences at speaking engagements, the truth was that he was filled with self-doubt. At events, he would speak about projecting positivity and overcoming adversity; but back in his hotel room or his home, he was struggling intensely.

J.R. had been so distracted with helping other soldiers deal with their own traumas that he wasn't paying enough attention to his own well-being. Instead, he was burying all of his emotions. He was suppressing an unhealthy amount of anger and resentment. And, like a pressure cooker, those emotions were about to explode in a way that would change his life once again.

His feelings of bitterness and resentment all came to a head one night in 2007 after a speaking engagement associated with the Indy 500 and a nonprofit veterans organization. J.R. was traveling back to the hotel with a fellow vet and friend named Dan Vargas as well as two other vets who were amputees. J.R. was sitting in the back of the SUV, watching the Indianapolis cityscape blur past his window. As the other guys in the SUV cracked sarcastic jokes, J.R. felt himself getting angrier and angrier, even though he couldn't explain why. It wasn't the jokes as much as the laughs—the fact that these guys were having fun and he was stewing in some unexplainable bitterness. His bad mood quickly turned combative, and it wasn't long before there was a physical altercation between J.R. and the other guys.

Dan Vargas pulled into the hotel parking lot and then managed to get J.R. alone in order to talk him down. Dan was straight with him: J.R. was no longer pleasant to be around. And he hadn't been for some time. Instead, J.R. just seemed angry. It was clear there was something that J.R. was bottling up inside, and he had to deal with it. Dan told J.R. to cry, to let it all out right there in the hotel parking lot. Of course, J.R. resisted, not wanting to appear vulnerable in front of a fellow soldier.

But then the tears came, whether J.R. wanted them to or not. He just kept crying, all his suppressed emotions rushing up out of him like a geyser. That's when J.R. realized just how much he had been keeping inside—all of the insecurities from his burns, all of the emotional trauma. It was all coming out. Also, there were long-buried issues from his youth—his father abandoning him, his mother's relationships with abusive men. J.R. had been forced to grow up so quickly that he hadn't dealt with all of the unresolved issues from his missed childhood.

That night in the hotel parking lot with Dan, J.R. learned what it truly meant to be vulnerable: to allow himself the space to deal with his emotions. It made all the difference in his life going forward. Although it didn't happen overnight, J.R. managed to shift his mindset and embrace a more lasting positivity by going through counselling and relying on friends and colleagues in the tough times, no longer shying away from vulnerability.

Sometime after that turning point, J.R. went out and got a tattoo. It was a cracked watch inked right on top of the unburned pale band left behind by the watch he was wearing on his wrist during the explosion. On the face of the tattooed watch, he had the date of the blast imprinted in roman numerals. He also put the time: 2:30 p.m. Strangely, or perhaps cosmically, what J.R. had come to learn was that almost exactly twenty years before that explosion, Maria had given birth to J.R. at 2:30 p.m. As J.R. explains, wounded vets call the day they were injured their "Alive Day." But for J.R., he considered it a rebirth.

In the process of that rebirth, J.R. had discovered ways to shape his pain into purpose, to turn lead into gold. In doing so, he found himself flush with opportunities.

One such opportunity was a chance to play a recurring role on the ABC daytime soap *All My Children*. When Dan had forwarded J.R. an email with a casting call for a wounded veteran to be featured on the soap opera, J.R. showed up for the audition, and to his surprise, he got the part. He had never acted in his life, but because he was able to tap into his real-life experiences and the genuine emotional vulnerability from his trauma, the producers cast him immediately. (While the role offered him a new spotlight for his cause and a host of fans, the greatest reward of that show was meeting his future wife, Diana, who worked for the executive producer.)

His time on *All My Children* led to another opportunity. Fans of the show started voicing enthusiasm for J.R. to be selected as a contestant on *Dancing with the Stars*, a dance competition show going into its tenth season. Again, J.R. had never professionally danced, but he had convinced himself to meet every opportunity with an open mind. He joined the cast of celebrity contestants and began training with his dance partner, Karina Smirnoff. To his shock, J.R. and Karina made it to the final round of the competition . . . and then they won it all. As J.R. remembers, "To think that eight years earlier I'd been leaning on my mom, trying to learn to walk again. Now I was a ballroom dancing champion."

Today, J.R. lives with his wife, Diana, and their young daughter. He has built a life and a home for himself that he never would have thought possible in those days, weeks, and months after the explosion in Iraq. In that home, J.R. has a Purple Heart from the military, he has memorabilia from his days on *All My Children*, and he has the Mirror Ball trophy from *Dancing with the Stars*. But the thing on his walls that he prizes most is a medal awarded to him by the secretary of the army, and it reads, "Outstanding Civilian Service." It recognizes his substantial contributions to his country off the battlefield. It's an honour that J.R. continues to earn every day as he brings awareness to wounded veterans and their struggle.

For J.R., *Alchemy* is about having the right mindset. And he believes it is *Alchemy* that has allowed him to be open to so many possibilities along his journey. As he says, "Underlying whatever it is you're going through, you have to remember that you, at the end of the day, are part of the possibility. You are the possibility. You're not the challenge; you are the possibility."

CHAPTER FOUR

Pioneer

_____

**"I have not failed. I've just found ten thousand
ways that don't work."**
—Thomas Edison

FEARLESS BELIEF

From a young age, Hugh Herr saw climbing
mountains as a pathway to a higher truth. For
him, the sport represented human achievement
in its purest form. In his early teens, Hugh
was conquering climbs that even skilled adults
wouldn't attempt. Along with his brothers, Hugh
spent much of his youth consuming any and all
literature on mountaineering, rock climbing, and
rescue techniques. Meanwhile, his parents would

take the family adventuring in the Canadian and American Rockies during their summer breaks. Even though all of the Herr boys climbed—and climbed well—it was the lanky, fair-haired Hugh who would first gain attention for his vertical abilities.

Hugh's earliest claim to fame came when, at only thirteen years old, he managed to climb one of the more challenging routes in the Shawangunk Mountains region. (Climbers often affectionately refer to this mountain range in the Mid-Atlantic as the "Gunks.") The Gunks is a popular climbing area with long bands of rock, typically ranging between two and four hundred feet, with large overhangs. Hugh would travel out to the Gunks at least once a week during climbing season. One day, he started up a route known as Persistent, an expert-grade climb that few could conquer (and which had a fitting name for Hugh). As he made his way up the rock, his mind and body worked together in harmony, reading the rock in such a precise way that he was able to "flash" the route, which is when a climber completes a route in one attempt, with no falls—an uncommon feat. It was a big moment for Hugh.

Word quickly spread that Hugh had flashed Persistent, and he earned a reputation as a climbing prodigy. The notice he received from that climb only encouraged Hugh to develop his abilities on the rock further, both in terms of his physicality and his philosophy. Physically, he was building his endurance, his flexibility, and his explosive strength. Philosophically, he was adopting a mental toughness that allowed him to accept the dark truth of climbing—a single error in movement could mean death.

By the time Hugh was seventeen, his relationship with climbing became an obsession, so much so that he even built in a three-hour break in his high school schedule so that he could climb each day. His grades in school may have suffered, but for Hugh, it was worth it. He was determined to become the world's greatest climber, no matter the consequences.

And had it not been for a fateful trek up Mount Washington in the middle of his junior year of high school, Hugh Herr very well may have achieved his lofty ambition.

In January 1982, Hugh and his climbing partner at the time, Jeff, had mapped out an ice-climbing adventure on Mount Washington, which boasts the highest peak in the Northeastern United States. The summit stands at over 6,200 feet, and the mountain—located in New Hampshire—is known for its erratic weather. Although it can be a moderately challenging endeavour in the spring and summer months, the mountain proves formidable in the winter as the wind whips up and icy snow makes for a treacherous climb. Since the mid-1800s, over one hundred people have died in that particular mountainous region, having fallen victim to avalanches, falling rocks, and heart-stopping temperatures. But Hugh had convinced himself that he was physically capable of completing any climb, anywhere; finishing even the hardest routes just required him to be strong in mind.

During the holiday break, Hugh and the twenty-year-old Jeff packed up all their gear and drove north for Mount Washington. From Hugh's hometown in rural Pennsylvania, it was a thirteen-hour drive (although a few wrong turns stretched it out to seventeen). In that car, they had only one cassette tape: The Police's *Reggatta de Blanc* album. They played it over and over and over again. As they sped north along the dark highway, the two young men belted out the lyrics at the top of their lungs—"Sending out an SOS! Sending out an SOS!"—until they finally reached their destination sometime after midnight.

Early the next morning, Hugh and Jeff set off up Mount Washington. With heavy snowfall in the forecast for later that day, Hugh wanted to get up to the summit before the weather turned. So, he left behind his sleeping bag in order to lighten his load. Hugh and Jeff moved briskly up the mountain, managing four ice pitches in an hour. But when they reached the summit, Hugh turned back and saw that the weather had worsened behind them, so they decided to head back down. However, there were two issues they had to contend with in their descent. First, on the way up the mountain, the wind was at their backs, and now it was coming right at their faces. The second issue was the topography of the summit, which had flat surfaces that made it easy to get disoriented. Suddenly, Hugh and Jeff found themselves in whiteout conditions, with sunset nearing, and they had no idea where the path was to get back down the mountain.

Before long, Hugh and Jeff were losing themselves deeper into the wilderness, their sense of direction frustrated by the blinding snow. With daylight fading and the snow picking up with the wind, they were fighting their way through chest-deep drifts, forced to make swimming motions to move through it. Since they couldn't see the ground, they had no idea what was beneath them. At one point, Hugh broke through a patch of ice and his legs fell into a stream with water coming up to his knees. His wet, freezing legs only made the disorienting trek harder for Hugh. As the sun disappeared completely, the two young men wondered if they would make it off the mountain alive.

For the next three days, Hugh and Jeff never saw another person on that mountain. The weather had kept other hikers and climbers away, which meant they were alone up there with no help in sight. By the end of that third day, with nightfall coming on, Hugh and Jeff could barely crawl through the snow. Their energy was sapped, and their bodies were suffering from hypothermia. At one point, Hugh shut his eyes and wished for death. As he lay there in the frozen blanket of snow, he was starting to accept his grim reality—nobody was coming to save them. And the song lyrics they had sung over and over again on the way north—"Sending out an SOS"—no doubt haunted him now.

Then, on the morning of the fourth day, a saving grace: a young woman who was out snowshoeing spotted Hugh and Jeff's tracks in the hardened snow. She followed the footprints until she could hear Jeff crying out for help. She quickly returned to town for reinforcements, and it wasn't long before an entire rescue team was on the scene. The two lost climbers were rushed to a nearby hospital for emergency medical attention.

At the hospital, both Hugh's and Jeff's parents were waiting anxiously for them. Unbeknownst to Hugh, there had been a massive rescue operation underway once the climbers hadn't returned a few nights earlier. In fact, one young man who had been part of the rescue effort had lost his life when an avalanche had thrown his body into a tree. (The remorse and guilt from the man's death would stay with Hugh to this day.) After the doctor examined Hugh, he told Hugh's parents that it was the worst case of frostbite he had seen in his twenty years of practicing medicine. In all likelihood, Hugh's legs would have to be amputated.

For several months following the incident, Hugh refused to accept the doctor's prognosis; he was determined to save his legs. However, the tissue around Hugh's ankles had rotted and become gangrenous, which meant amputation was the only option. When he woke from the surgery, Hugh looked down and saw there was nothing left below his knees. His first reaction was shock. Then a storm of sadness and loss struck him. For the next few months, he was awash in grief for the loss of a life he thought he was going to have but was now gone.

Once the shock wore off and his knees healed, Hugh went to a rehab centre, where he was fitted for two prostheses. As Hugh struggled to move around on his new limbs, he asked the doctor what he would be able to do now that he had artificial legs. The doctor said he'd be able to get around without a cane one day and perhaps even drive a car with hand controls. As for climbing—the one thing that motivated Hugh, the one thing he lived for—those days were over, according to the doctor.

Of course, the same grit and determination that once pushed Hugh to great heights on the rock would now serve him in his new adversity. Hugh decided to dismiss the doctor's assessment that he would never climb again. Within months of having his legs amputated, Hugh convinced his older brother, Tony, to take him climbing.

One afternoon, Hugh and Tony drove to Safe Harbor along the Susquehanna, where Hugh walked unsteadily along the railroad tracks that led to Tailrace, a medium-grade climb. As Hugh and his brother walked along the rails, Hugh felt pain in his knees. The plaster in his prostheses would often crack, and it made walking uncomfortable. However, once Hugh reached the rock and began clambering over boulders, the pain subsided. He was still weak and he wasn't climbing like he used to, but for the first time in a long time, Hugh felt like himself again.

That first attempt at climbing after having his legs amputated opened his eyes to a new perspective—Hugh wasn't disabled, the technology was. He knew he could climb—he just needed a more advanced and targeted prosthetic limb to compensate for his missing legs. And he had a *fearless belief* that he could invent his way to a better life for himself, one that would allow him to keep climbing even with his new adversity.

So, Hugh set to work on designing new and improved prostheses. Even without a science or math background (and still finishing up high school), Hugh's passion drove him to create workable solutions. He used his knowledge of rock climbing to help shape his artificial limbs. He made them longer to optimize his height for the climbs; he crafted interchangeable foot features that he could swap out depending on the surface of the rock. Over the next six months, there was a lot of trial and error, but the results of his mechanical contrivances were astounding. As he says, "At the beginning of that year, society said I was broken. One year later, I had surpassed my pre-amputation climbing abilities and done climbs no climber had ever done."

Hugh's passion and his inspiring story drew plenty of attention, and in May 1983, he was featured on the cover of *Outside* magazine. On that cover, Hugh is perched on a rock, arms folded, with his array of interchangeable feet sitting between his two prosthetic limbs. (It's worth Googling the cover image just for the sheer sense of accomplishment in Hugh's face and to see his designs.) Even though this moment may have felt like the climax of Hugh's story and his success, there would actually be much more to come. Hugh's passion for innovation— sparked by his own personal adversity—would lead to a higher purpose, one that would touch the lives of people spanning the globe.

But before we get to that, let's take a look at the Life Element that helped Hugh power through his challenges.

DEFINING PIONEER

In Reach, you selected a goal that will push you outside of your comfort zone. By taking on that challenge, you are inherently also welcoming adversity into your life. The Pioneer element is a tool and a mindset to help you tackle the challenges you have accepted by embracing this learning opportunity. It boils down to this: *To Pioneer is to fearlessly use an innovator's mindset to solve complex challenges.*

Think about Pioneer in the context of Hugh Herr. After his legs were amputated, he was caught in a storm of self-doubt and grief. But then, he did the hard thing. He turned into the storm. He decided that even with his legs now gone, he was going to find a way to climb again, perhaps even better than he had before. That became his Vision. And facing the rock again for the first time—attempting to climb it even with rudimentary prostheses—that was his Reach. Now, when he started to innovate and use his own creativity to solve the challenge—that was Pioneering.

The same goes for Mandy Harvey. Think back to the moment in her story where she realized she could sing even though she was deaf. Even though she could hold a tune with her father in her basement, performing on a stage with a band accompanying her was a far greater challenge. In order to keep tempo with the band, she would have to be able to hear the beat. But how was that possible since she was deaf? In this case, Mandy tapped into her creative thinking to solve the problem. By going barefoot on the stage and by keeping one hand on the lid of the piano, she could feel the vibrations and, in turn, the rhythm. In a sense, her hands and feet became her ears. This is Pioneering.

You may be thinking, "Sure, they could Pioneer, but that's because they're creative and I'm not." Many people believe that being highly creative is something you are born with. That it's a rare gift. But we're here to tell you that it's actually quite common. In fact, creativity and ingenuity are both inside of you already; you just need to tap into them. The truth is, being creative is really an emotional attribute. It's about fearlessness and about belief. It's about persevering through what will likely be many failures and successes as you slowly make your way toward your solution.

As Hugh Herr says, "Pioneer is a fearless belief in a future that does not yet exist."

WHY PIONEER MATTERS

If you can't learn to Pioneer, you'll never break through the adversities you're facing and create a new future. When you learn to trust that you too can be a Pioneer, you start to become fearless in your pursuit of your goal.

So, here's what you need to know.

You're going to fail—the key is to learn from it. Your Vision for yourself is big and bold. Your Reach goal is stretching you out of your comfort zone. Guess what? This means you're going to fail. Although most of us are never going to like failure, we have to start seeing it as a form of progress. We have to embrace failure as a learning opportunity. We have to limit failure's ability to make us give up. Think of it in the same terms Edison did: "I have not failed. I've just found ten thousand ways that won't work."

You'll also need different perspectives to succeed. When confronted with an opportunity or challenge, we're going to need to reach out to others on our Rope Team (see chapter 5) who can provide input, ideas, and guidance. For most problems we encounter, there's probably someone else out there who can make our solution even better than we could make it if we do it on our own. Our Pioneering solutions are really built on the backs of others' successes. So, we need to learn to identify experts, ask good questions, and assume we don't have all the answers. As we gather input, we'll amalgamate into a creative solution.

You'll be resource constrained. We always are. Resource constraints only fuel your creativity as you get the most out of limited resources. Great pioneers marshal diverse resources to successfully achieve your goals, often finding solutions where others might have given up.

You may need to try lots of things before you find the right solution. You need to learn to experiment to find solutions. You need to tinker—learning through both successes and failures to quickly improve your ideas. You iterate quickly, moving from one prototype to the next, knowing that the end product will be better and better with each successive step. You do not seek perfection because you know it rarely exists and that a ninety per cent solution is often all you need to have a terrific product, service, or idea. You introduce new ways of looking at problems and often use design thinking to rapidly innovate, test assumptions, pivot, and move forward. Remember Mandy's story: she spends countless hours practicing her music and techniques to learn to be on pitch.

In our own program, we ask our participants to rate themselves on the accuracy of this statement: "I am able to focus on solutions rather than problems." They rate it before and after they have participated in the program, and remarkably, our research shows fifty per cent more participants are able to be solutions focused once they've learned to Pioneer. "The No Barriers program showed me that no matter the problem, you can overcome it using creative solutions," shared one student participant.

The bottom line: if you want to fearlessly pursue your Vision and your Reach goals, you'll need to Pioneer. It's just that simple.

Grand Philosopher #1
Design Thinking from Stanford D.school

Design thinking is a modern approach to the creative process, and it embraces the idea that everybody has the capacity to be innovative. By thinking like a designer—and by having access to the same toolkit as designers—you will be able to create solutions to your hardest problems.

The concepts that make up design thinking are rooted in a deep history of innovators. In the 1970s and 1980s, the ideas of design thinking have been moulded into something that just makes simple sense, and it is the go-to model to teach yourself the skills to be creative. For our purposes, we take a look at one of the most influential voices in design thinking, which is Stanford University's d.school.

At Stanford d.school, their focus has been developing creative confidence while also providing a structured approach to creating new ideas. They believe that design should start with what humans need, what has the most use for us, and what is emotionally meaningful.

Through their program, they emphasize the importance of being a lifelong learner, and they lay out the tools that can help you through the creative process. As they say, "Design thinking gives you faith in your creative abilities and a process for transforming difficult challenges into opportunities for design."

The design process at the d.school relies on five phases. At No Barriers, we have found their step-process approach useful in guiding people as they Pioneer through their own adversities.

Below, we summarize the d.school's design methodology:

1. *Discovery.* Here is where you identify your challenge and state it clearly. By understanding what your challenge is, you can determine how to approach it and what you need to research.

2. *Interpretation.* Through your research, whether by reading or consulting experts on the subject, you have gathered information. Now you have to interpret what is meaningful and most helpful in that information.

3. *Ideation.* It's time to start generating ideas through a brainstorming process. At the start of this phase, no idea is a bad idea. Don't discount anything. Then, after you have collected your possible solutions, refine those ideas with the best potential.

4. *Experimentation.* This is where you roll up your sleeves and get your hands dirty. Let your ideas take shape by designing prototypes or trying them out. One of the key elements to this phase is taking in feedback.

5. *Evolution.* You've tried something new; now how do you improve it? Use that feedback you gathered in the Experimentation phase to help you improve on your idea.

A little bit later, we'll guide you through these five steps in a way that will allow it to be more specific to your particular journey and adversity. But for now, just take note of the general concepts here, and internalize the key to design thinking. It's having the confidence to know that there are solutions out there to your problem, and while you may not find them on your first attempt, you will find them.

Grand Philosopher #2
Carol Dweck

Back in the early 1980s, Dr. Carol Dweck was working in the fields of social and developmental psychology when her research pointed her to two distinct learning personality traits—while some people rebound after failure, others become distressed by even the smallest setback. This key observation inspired Dr. Dweck to further study these distinct personalities, and her research led her to simple but ground-breaking ideas that have become foundational for the Pioneer element.

Over the course of several decades, Dr. Dweck and her colleagues studied thousands of students to better understand these opposing learning traits, and what she discovered was that many students saw failure as a fundamental character flaw. "I failed at this, I just can't do it, and I'll never be able to be good at it," they would think. They had what Dr. Dweck called a fixed mindset— they didn't believe they could grow and develop in an area because they thought there was something fundamental about their intelligence, their character, or their personality that would never change.

From her book *Mindset: The New Psychology of Success*, Dweck described her findings this way:

> In the **fixed mindset**, everything is about the outcome. If you fail—or if you're not the best—it's all been wasted. The **growth mindset** allows people to value what they're doing regardless of the outcome. They're tackling problems, charting new courses, working on important issues. Maybe they haven't found the cure for cancer, but the search was deeply meaningful.

Does this sound familiar? How often have you put pressure on yourself to get it exactly right the first time? And when you don't get the outcome you want, you simply give up because you think, "Well, maybe I just don't have that skill." When we have a fixed mindset—when we believe that intelligence and ability are only innate—we don't allow ourselves to grow.

The goal of the Pioneer element is to move you from a fixed mindset to a growth mindset. People who have a growth mindset believe their talents can be developed through hard work, input from others, research, and/or planning. They worry less about being smart and more about learning, growing, and innovating. By adopting a growth mindset, you can do away with your fear of failure and start to see it as a step toward success.

And this leads to another influential idea in Carol Dweck's research: *the power of yet*. In her TED Talk, Dr. Dweck discusses how the phrase "not yet" can be a powerful tool in your ability to grow. At the beginning of the talk, she highlights a school in Chicago where students were not given failing grades when they didn't pass a class; instead, they were given a grade of "Not Yet." She continues, "If you get a failing grade, you think 'I'm nothing, I'm nowhere.' But if you get the grade 'Not Yet,' you understand that you're on a learning curve. It gives you a path into the future."

So, as you practice Pioneering and continue on your journey in overcoming your challenges, remember that abilities can be developed through persistence. Also remember, when you fail, just keep telling yourself, "Not yet."

PIONEER IN PRACTICE
J.K. Rowling

No doubt, you are familiar with J.K. Rowling's rags-to-riches story, going from a single mother without enough money to put food on the table to publishing the endlessly popular *Harry Potter* series and becoming one of the wealthiest women in the world. It's an inspiring story even just in that one line, but it is within the details of her journey that you can find the essence of what it means to Pioneer.

Since a young age, J.K. Rowling had wanted to be an author, writing short stories even at six years old that impressed her friends and family. But her path from a young aspiring scribe to a successful author was not so clean and linear. There were years and years of uncertainty and self-doubt in between.

In a 2008 Harvard commencement speech, Rowling talks honestly about some of the hardest miles of her journey. Seven years after she had graduated college, she had failed on a grand scale: "An exceptionally short-lived marriage had imploded, and I was jobless, a lone parent, and poor as it is possible to be in modern Britain without being homeless." While Rowling's vision for herself was to become a published author, poverty was standing in her way.

In that poverty lived fear and humiliation; there also lived a deep depression. Rowling has said that it was in those darker days that she had contemplated suicide more than once. Repeated failures, both in her personal and professional life, had left her feeling empty. But over time, she began to see the benefits of her failures. As she says, "Failure meant a stripping away of the inessential. I stopped pretending to myself that I was anything other than what I was and began to direct all my energy into finishing the only work that mattered to me."

Rowling started to use her daughter's nap time to write. Each day, as her daughter slept in the stroller next to her at a coffee shop, Rowling would chip away at what would become *Harry Potter and the Philosopher's Stone*. For both her and her daughter, she was driven by a fearless belief in a world that did not exist yet: both the imaginary world of

Harry Potter that she was bringing to life on the page and the actual future world where Rowling hoped to no longer live in poverty. That fearlessness is what allowed her to submit her first few chapters to publishers. After countless rejections, Rowling finally found a publisher interested in the story she wanted to tell . . . and the rest is Wizarding World history.

A final thought on J.K. Rowling: She has said, "You will never truly know yourself or the strength of your friendships until both have been tested by adversity." As you think of ways to Pioneer, keep that second part of her statement in mind as well. Who are those friends or colleagues or mentors who can help you as you try to innovate your way through your challenges? Realizing you're not alone can play a critical part in giving you the confidence you'll need to push forward.

Nerissa Cannon

When Nerissa Cannon was in her junior year of college, she unexpectedly and inexplicably began to lose her mobility. Nerissa started to experience chronic pain, which was making it difficult for her to walk. At first, she ignored the symptoms, hoping her pain would pass as quickly as it came. But as her pain progressively worsened, she sought the opinion of a doctor.

After the first doctor couldn't explain the source of Nerissa's pain or why she was losing her mobility, Nerissa visited another doctor and then another. No answers. She then went to several specialists, undergoing test after test. Still nothing. After several years of consultations and tests, every doctor and specialist came up empty: nobody could give an answer to why Nerissa's body and her abilities were deteriorating.

While growing up, Nerissa had spent most of her time outdoors, engaging in sports and hiking through nature. Suddenly, that no longer felt possible. Nerissa was losing not only her mobility but also a sense of who she was in this world now reframed by her new adversity. As she became untethered from her identity, Nerissa sank into a profoundly deep and unrelenting depression.

As Nerissa recounts:

I confided in a close friend that I was done. I couldn't see past my despair and loss, and I no longer wanted to live. Who was I if I couldn't do what brought me fulfilment? My friend somehow persuaded me to hold out for another six months. She told me if I felt the same in six months, I could end my pain, and she would understand. I decided to commit to this deadline.

With her own self-imposed clock ticking away, Nerissa decided she didn't want to simply give up. Instead, she would continue searching for answers. One day during that six-month period, Nerissa was made aware of the No Barriers community. She applied to the program and was pleasantly surprised to be chosen for a scholarship to the No Barriers Summit. As she immersed herself in the activities of the weekend-long summit, she was able to see herself through the eyes of others, and this new perspective offered a new truth—she needed to see herself for what she had to offer, rather than what she lacked. The experience made her feel like she had purpose and potential. She was excited for life again.

Another key takeaway from the summit: Nerissa had been so focused on searching for *why* she was losing her mobility, that she had been avoiding *how* she could cope with her new adversity. And at No Barriers, she found the answer to that question: *Pioneer*.

In the weeks and months that followed the summit, Nerissa used the knowledge and support system she had found in her No Barriers community to help her achieve things she would have thought impossible before that experience—kayaking, hiking, and rock climbing among the activities. For her, the thing that had been holding her back was her fear of failing. As she says, "The fear of failing can keep us stuck. It often keeps me stuck. Nelson Mandela once said, 'I never lose. I either win or learn.' But in that principle is always forward momentum. ALWAYS. You can't win or learn standing still. You can only grow through movement."

With her confidence buoyed, Nerissa took on an even greater challenge: hiking her first 14er (a mountain that reaches elevation above fourteen thousand feet). In association with a No Barriers program called What's Your

Everest, Nerissa and a team of twenty-seven other people (including Erik Weihenmayer) set out one September morning before the sun was even up, embarking on the seven-mile uphill journey. With Nerissa in an all-terrain wheelchair with levers, she could make it up much of the path on her own. But there were also plenty of moments of towing, spotting, and carrying along the way. Five hours later, Nerissa and her team had reached the summit, a testament to collaboration and grit and also to Pioneering.

That experience has made a profound impact on Nerissa's life, and she continues to live an active life in the outdoors in spite of her restricted mobility. As Nerissa says, "Since getting involved with the No Barriers Summit, I've learned how to be creative in using what abilities I do have. I'm more active now than I ever have been."

BECOMING A PIONEER

Start with your Vision. Does your Vision excite you? Can you picture yourself once you've achieved it? To be a great Pioneer, you have to have a fearless belief in a world that does not yet exist. Your Vision should be a guiding force here. It will help you break through failures and missteps. If your Vision is not inspiring you to be fearless, you may need to reframe it.

Next, work on your mindset. Remember Dr. Carol Dweck's framing of the *fixed mindset* versus the *growth mindset*? See if you can recognize the fixed mindset in how you have faced challenges in the past, or even how you conduct yourself in your daily routine. Do you sometimes avoid challenges, or give up easily when confronted by challenges? If someone criticizes you, do you ignore that criticism rather than looking for morsels of truth that might be helpful? Or, when you see someone else in your life experience success, do you resent that success or feel threatened by it?

If you can see yourself in any of these traits of the fixed mindset, then to some degree, you have a deterministic view of the world, and that can be holding you back from your full potential. We want you to shift your mindset to one in which you have a greater sense of free will. With the growth mindset, you will embrace challenges, see the value in learning from criticism, and appreciate the lessons from other people's successes.

Now that you understand the fundamentals of the growth mindset, you'll need to practice this new way of thinking. It turns out our brains are malleable, so you can train your brain to think of challenges and setbacks as learning opportunities.

Try this:

Revisit your Roadmap you made in chapter 2. As you go through the goals you wrote in order to get you to your Vision, on a separate piece of paper, make a list of any negative inner thoughts you tell yourself for each goal. (For example, if you have a negative inner voice around the idea of learning how to knit, "I don't have the time to learn a new skill.")

Have you done that?

Okay, now refute that list. Next to each negative inner thought, write your own fearless response that demonstrates why you CAN do this and write them down. (For example, "I will take thirty minutes each day after I eat my lunch to make time for me to learn to knit.") By the end of this exercise, you will have gained an understanding that while there are many doubts and reasons why you may fail, there are also many creative ideas and courageous solutions for you to succeed and achieve your goals.

Now you're ready to start the design thinking process. Earlier, we outlined Stanford d.school's five-step structured approach to creating new ideas. It's time for you to consider those steps in relation to your own Pioneering efforts.

1. *Discovery.* Go out and talk to people about your challenge. Learn from them. Ask good questions. Get outside your own head and invite others in. When you're faced with a new challenge, you often think that you're the only one who can solve it. You're going to be surprised when you start talking to people about how many folks have been through similar challenges. This requires you, of course, to be vulnerable—to open up and share your Reach and what challenge you're facing. If you're not ready to talk about your challenge with others, another great technique

for discovery is to just try things. For Nerissa Cannon, this act of trying was reaching out to No Barriers.

2. *Interpretation.* Search for meaning behind what you've learned through your discovery process. Create a narrative that helps you frame your challenge with your newfound insight. Has it changed what you think your challenge really is? Sometimes as we talk to more people, we reframe our challenge in a new way. What's the real problem you're trying to solve? As Einstein said, "If I were given one hour to save the planet, I would spend fifty-nine minutes defining the problem and one minute resolving it."

3. *Ideation.* Now that you have a new perspective, come up with a list of ways you might tackle your Reach. Go for volume—keep yourself open to all the possibilities no matter how crazy they seem at first. Don't get stuck on any one idea. You want to generate as many ways as you can. Try to think outside the box.

4. *Experimentation.* Now look at your list of solutions and choose just one that you'd like to try. Remember, it might not work and that's okay. You have a *growth mindset*. You know that through failure you can learn, too.

5. *Evolution.* Assess what you've learned. Pivot if necessary.

This is a process that you will return to over and over again as you try to create solutions to each new challenge that presents itself as you move closer toward your Vision. Accept that the process demands patience and an open mind, and it will serve you well in your journey.

Now that you've had a chance to practice this Life Element, let's rejoin Hugh Herr in his story of Pioneering.

GREATER HEIGHTS

While Hugh had managed to Pioneer his artificial legs and feet in ways that allowed him to climb again—a large part of his Vision—he was still experiencing problems with one specific aspect of the prosthetics—the socket where his kneecap met the artificial limb was causing him pain. A lot of pain. And this would often keep him off his feet. So now Hugh had a specific question he needed to answer: "Is there a different kind of socket that would allow me to walk with less pain?"

As Hugh set out to answer this question, he realized he didn't yet have the requisite skills in math and science he was going to need. In fact, Hugh was so focused on climbing during high school that he had graduated without even understanding basic math like percentages. But he did have grit and determination, as well as a mind that had been exercised for years on the rock when Hugh would have to make quick mental calculations, recognize patterns and sequences, and creatively engineer his way upward. So, if Hugh was going to solve the challenge of his prosthetic socket, he was going to need the academic and technical know-how.

In what could be referred to as a Reach moment, Hugh enrolled at a nearby college, Millersville University. There, he got a crash course in anatomy, and he tailored his curriculum around the physics and mechanics that would be involved in engineering his new socket. Over the next several years, Hugh studied relentlessly. He began experimenting with various stump-receiving sockets, testing out new adhesives and materials to see what would ease his pain. His tireless efforts to invent his way through his adversity would lead to a patent for a new socket, one that was easier on his knee. He also earned himself a new nickname in his climbing and academic communities: Mechanical Boy.

In only a few short years, Hugh went from being unable to take ten per cent of hundred to understanding the foundations of quantum mechanics—all because he had a burning question that he had to answer. But learning about and experimenting with prosthetics also taught him how much more progress still needed to be made in the field. So, following his undergraduate studies and his patented socket, Hugh would go on to study mechanical engineering at MIT and then continue at Harvard, where he earned a PhD in biophysics.

Today, Hugh Herr heads up the Biomechatronics group at the MIT Media Lab, and he is widely praised for the advancements he has made in his field, which marries human physiology and electromechanics. He develops bionic legs that augment human walking and running, and one of his most notable innovations is a computer-controlled artificial knee. In 2011, *Time* magazine coined him "The Leader of the Bionic Age." In 2018, he took to the TED stage to share his bold vision for a future without disability: "During the twilight years of this century, I believe humans will be unrecognizable in morphology and dynamics from what we are today. Humanity will take flight and soar."

You can almost see the straight line between his original Vision—to create prosthetics that allowed him to climb to great heights once again—and his Vision now, which may sound more ambitious but still involves upgrading the human body so that it can one day go higher than it ever has.

And here's the important takeaway: Hugh's Vision and his efforts to Pioneer that Vision have evolved to be about more than just himself. While Hugh's journey started in a very personal place as he struggled for his own survival, his resulting innovations are helping people all across the globe. Oftentimes, it's the most personal motivations that can lead to your journey having the greatest impact on the lives of others.

Finally, it's worth noting how Hugh speaks about the Pioneer element. For him, the true Pioneer has two characteristics, which he applies in his life on a daily basis. The first is the belief that there is a solution to every problem. The only way you will keep searching for an answer is if you truly believe it's out there waiting to be discovered. And the second characteristic is outright *grit*. For him, the only way you're going to continue to find solutions is if you commit yourself to the journey and never give up.

CHAPTER FIVE

Rope Team

"I get by with a little help from my friends."
—John, Paul, George, and Ringo

THE SOUNDLESS JOURNEY HOME

Here's the first thought that crosses your mind when you meet Command Sergeant Major Gretchen Evans: *This woman has stories to tell.* You can see it in her eyes—a stoicism that makes her appear taller than her five-foot-two stature. You can hear it in her manner of speaking— an economy of language in which every word serves a purpose. And you can sense it in her demeanour—a hard-earned confidence that comes only once someone has already endured so many of the slings and arrows that life has in store for them.

Gretchen Evans's stories come from her twenty-seven-year career in the army, and they are filled with the trials and traumas of combat, as well as the sand and soil collected from more countries than you can count on two hands. And through all of her experiences, there runs a consistent theme—to get through our greatest adversities, we must often depend on the support of others.

"I don't know whether the army found me or I found the army, but we were a perfect match." This is how Gretchen describes her origins in the military. The clearest detail for her is that she was a young woman from Abilene, Texas, who had lost her father at the age of fifteen, and she was looking for a way to make it on her own in the world. She enlisted in the army with the intention of getting her head right and her back straight, a way to support herself while finding a purpose. And purpose she found. For Gretchen, the best part of being a soldier was that she worked until the sergeant major told her that her day was over. There was simplicity and clarity in that. Yes, a soldier gives up much of their freedom in the military, but in exchange, they are given structure and a sense of purpose.

Gretchen's earliest years in the military were spent in the intelligence field. After basic training, she attended intelligence school in Arizona before being stationed in Germany. There, she worked mostly off-grid in civilian clothes, analysing other armies and collecting intel on how they operated. Then, after a stint in Italy running counterintelligence, Gretchen decided she didn't want to be on the bench and away from the action anymore, so she went on to airborne school. She joined up with the elite 82nd Airborne at Fort Bragg in North Carolina. It wasn't long before she was deployed to conflict zones in the West Indies, in South America, in the Middle East, and elsewhere around the globe.

Gretchen had both the mettle and the mindset that made her well suited for the army, more so than she had imagined when she first enlisted. In fact, even though Gretchen had not intended to make a career out of the army, she continued to find reasons to stay. After her initial four-year enlistment ended, she said, "Okay, I'll do four more." Then eight years in the army turned into twelve. And, as Gretchen says, once you have been in the army for twelve years, you have fully embraced the life. As she was shipped off to places like Iraq, Afghanistan, Bosnia, and Somalia, Gretchen made a name for herself as a soldier who could be relied on and also one who could lead with honour. (As Gretchen likes to say, "We are soldiers. If nothing else, we are our word.") Her dedication and her innate leadership skills helped her rise through the ranks to command sergeant major, the highest enlisted rank in the army.

In her new role, Gretchen was no longer just getting her purpose from the army; she was also giving a sense of purpose to other soldiers. It felt good. But it also felt freighted with far more responsibility. The stakes were so much higher for her personally. People's lives were now in her hands. And nothing would underscore this new reality more than a fatal drive from Kabul to Bagram during one of her many tours of duty in Afghanistan.

The main road between Kabul and Bagram is named Jalalabad Road, and it is one of the more perilous journeys that US soldiers can make in that part of Afghanistan. One morning, Gretchen and her security team drove the thirty miles to Bagram, where Gretchen attended a meeting with her higher-ups. As Gretchen and her team prepared for their return trip later that day, Gretchen was asked to transport two airmen—who had just landed from the States—back to Kabul. Gretchen agreed to the request, and she put one of the airmen into her Humvee, while the other followed in the Humvee behind hers.

About twelve miles into the trip back to Kabul, as Gretchen had her mind focused on a brief from the meeting she had just attended, her convoy started receiving small arms fire. "Three o'clock, 100 yards, exit left!" the gunner yelled down from the top of the vehicle. Gretchen immediately ordered the airman next to her to get out of the vehicle before rockets started flying. The airman obeyed, but instead of staying low as he exited—as one should when under fire—the airman simply stepped from the Humvee, and he was shot instantly. Gretchen ducked out of the vehicle and then covered the airman to protect him. But it was too late: the airman was already dead.

A quick response force arrived within minutes, and Gretchen and her team were given cover as they loaded into an Apache helicopter. In the hours that followed,

Gretchen ran through the attack in her mind, trying to figure out how things went so wrong so quickly. What she realized was that the airmen had not been provided ammo for their weapons. While this was standard operating procedure, the request for transport had already deviated from the usual procedure; this, perhaps, had left Gretchen's security team unprepared.

In addition, Gretchen had her head in a brief instead of on the perilous drive, and this left her feeling like she was partially responsible for the death of the airman. As she recounts in her memoir, *Leading from the Front*, "Why was I reading on one of the most dangerous roads in Afghanistan? Why did I not at least lean over and ask this Airman his name and shake his hand? . . . It would have only taken a minute to put him at ease, had I just taken the time to talk to him. I had failed at the one thing I said I would never do as a CSM. I put stuff over troops. I hated myself for this selfish act." As they arrived back at their base in Kabul, Gretchen made a grim observation: the airman, who had just landed earlier that day from the States, had not even had the chance to unpack his bags.

For Gretchen, that incident with the airman stuck with her. She would count it among one of her toughest days in the army. As she says, it kept her up at night and stripped the flavour from her food for a long time to come.

But while there were tough days that planted seeds of doubt in Gretchen, she was surrounded by people who could understand what she was going through. One such person was Robert, a colleague of hers who served as the senior chaplain for all of Afghanistan. Gretchen and Robert became great friends during one of her deployments to the Middle East, and the two of them cultivated a deep mutual respect for each other as they dealt with the worst and the best of war.

Then, during a time when Robert was off at another duty station in the Middle East, Gretchen received a letter from Robert, and it centred on a question: *Did Gretchen think she could ever be romantically interested in him?* Her first reaction was to come up with all the reasons that a relationship between her and Robert just would not work—he was in the navy and she was in the army; he was an officer, and she was a non-commissioned officer; and both of them had years left to serve.

But then, during a visit back to the States for some R & R, Gretchen spent some time with Robert away from the sounds and sights of the war front, and they discussed what a life together might look like. And this helped Gretchen see the upsides of a romantic relationship with Robert. Perhaps most importantly, Robert understood the stresses of Gretchen's job, and he knew the daily dangers that she faced. By the end of Gretchen's visit, Robert proposed, and Gretchen said yes. The following day, Gretchen flew back to Afghanistan to finish her tour of duty. Once her tour was over, she planned to return to the United States to marry Robert.

As a garrison command major sergeant, Gretchen was an advocate for the soldiers in Afghanistan. On behalf of the general, Gretchen would visit troops at different bases and check in on them. Essentially, she served as a filter between the soldiers and their commander, making sure that morale was where it should be. On one such visit—about six months after Robert had proposed—Gretchen was at a forward operating base speaking with soldiers when the base came under heavy mortar fire. Gretchen yelled at the troops, ordering them back to the bunkers. As rockets exploded around her, she realized that they were under attack by a suicide team—enemy fighters who were willing to give up their own lives just to take out the military base. Suddenly, a rocket hit ten yards to her right, and the blast flung Gretchen some thirty feet before she crashed into a concrete bunker.

Her world went black.

When Gretchen regained consciousness in a hospital in Germany, the first thing she did was a body check, looking to make sure she still had all her limbs. To her relief, they were all there. Then a doctor entered, and he was holding a small white board. On it, he wrote, "You're deaf." He was right, she realized—there was no sound in the room. Nothing. Gretchen took the board from the doctor, wiped away the words he had written, and then she wrote her own word: "Forever?" The doctor nodded.

The impact of the blast had blown out her eardrums and given Gretchen a traumatic brain injury. For that reason, Gretchen knew immediately that her military career was over. In her decades of service up to that point, she had learned that a broken soldier is no longer a good soldier. Perhaps that's not fair, but Gretchen knew it was the truth. If anything, Gretchen was pragmatic, but it still hurt.

When Gretchen thinks back on that moment, she sees parallels in the story of the Scarecrow from *The Wizard of Oz*. Toward the end of the film, Dorothy, the Lion, the Tin Man, and the Scarecrow have defeated the Wicked Witch of the West and they have the Emerald City in their sights. Then the flying monkeys show up for one final assault—they tear into the Scarecrow, ripping out his stuffing. As the monkeys fly off, the Scarecrow is left there on the Yellow Brick Road, his stuffing scattered about. He's powerless.

Lying there in her hospital bed, Gretchen felt like the Scarecrow. She had seen the rewards of her journey right ahead of her, and then the flying monkeys came for her in the form of suicide attackers. And they took everything away from her. The blast had stripped her not only of her hearing but also her sense of self. The army was in her blood. It was her purpose. *Who would she be now?*

And, of course, there was Robert. She was engaged to someone who had proposed to her before her injuries. *Was he going to want her like this? Was it even fair to ask that of him?* As she recovered in the hospital in Germany, she spoke with Robert over the phone. She told him that he was under no obligation to keep the proposal he had made six months earlier. Gretchen would understand if he did not want to move forward with the wedding.

A week later, Gretchen returned to US soil. Along with other soldiers, she entered a gymnasium at Fort

Sam Houston, where family and friends were awaiting their arrival. Gretchen, who still had a bandage wrapped around her head, was carrying the colours of her unit. As she moved further into the gym, she looked around for Robert, but she couldn't find his face.

Her heart sank, and she sighed. She didn't blame Robert for not being there, but it was hard not to feel alone. It was difficult to comprehend how she was going to move forward and mend without support from others.

In the aftermath of the flying monkeys attack, the Scarecrow had the help of Dorothy, the Lion, and the Tin Man to put his stuffing back inside him. *Who was going to help put the stuffing back inside Gretchen?*

DEFINING ROPE TEAM

At No Barriers, a *Rope Team* is a group of people you trust, who are linked together to encourage you and your Vision. It's a support system you can't live without. The term originally comes from high-altitude mountain climbing, where it describes a group of people joined by a climbing rope and thus secured against falling. If a climber slips on a slope, others on the team self-arrest and act as the human anchors to stop the fall. Team members then work together to rescue the fallen climber.

Even if you aren't a climber on a high-altitude mountain, you still face challenges in your life, and you know how important it is to have a team of people in your life who you can trust and count on. They are people you can't live without, supporting you to overcome the obstacles in your way and move toward your Vision.

At the core of this Life Element is the notion that it is nearly impossible to achieve your Vision by yourself, let alone make it through your life journey with a smile on your face. You depend on others for many things. In this chapter, we will cover the critical aspects of creating your Rope Team, including the importance of friendship, the role of trust in any friendship, and the secrets to building team effectiveness.

Because we have a tendency to use the term "friend" rather loosely to cover an array of relationships—from the guy who lived across the hall from you in college ten years ago, to the parents of your children's friends that you interact with on social media, to the person you talk to once a week about your biggest challenges and your life vision—we want to narrow the definitional scope for this chapter.

Ask yourself, who are those friends you can genuinely rely on? Who would take you in if you didn't have a place to stay for the night? Which friends are willing to struggle alongside you? Or as Gretchen Evans might frame the question: *Which friends would you call your battle buddies?*

This chapter will focus on building what we call **On-Rope friends**: those people in your life you are deeply interconnected to; people who support your Vision (and you, theirs); people who, if they vanished, your life satisfaction would noticeably decrease. "Your tribe determines your vibe," as Robin Roberts likes to say. In this chapter, we want to make sure you have the right tribe to help you overcome your adversity.

WHY ROPE TEAM MATTERS

If a friend told you that he or she was going to climb Mount Everest alone, you would likely sit that friend down and tell them they weren't thinking clearly. You might ask them: *What would happen if you got stranded on your own? Who would help you up if you fell? Don't you want someone along who has done the climb before, someone who can point out the pitfalls ahead?* Obviously, it would be reckless and irresponsible to attempt such a perilous climb without a group of experienced and supportive climbers.

While Erik Weihenmayer *actually* climbed Mount Everest and used an *actual* rope team in that expedition, each of the other people we have profiled in this book also understood the value of a support system as they navigated their own journeys. Mandy Harvey had her father and her vocal coach to not just cheer her on but also to help her develop her voice. J.R. Martinez had, among other people, his good friend Dan Vargas, who prompted J.R. to look inward and confront the struggles of his past in order to move forward. They learned that while the stakes might not seem as though they always rise to the level of high-altitude climbing, having a rope team of friends is no less significant in our daily lives.

In his 2004 book *Vital Friends: The People You Can't Afford to Live Without*, author Tom Rath studies the impact of friendship in relation to some of our most difficult adversities—divorce, homelessness, depression, and a sense of malaise at work. Through interviews, Rath discovered that more often than not, people credited lack of genuine friendship as the root of their diminished personal and professional health. Rath, whose aim in the book is to bolster the reader's sense of wellness, recommends surrounding yourself with people who will champion your efforts, who will open your mind to new ideas, and who will energize you.

But friends don't just have an impact on our personal happiness and our work life; they also impact our physical health. In 2001, researchers at Duke University Medical Center studied the protective qualities of friendship on people with heart disease. The people who had lesser quality friendships were twice as likely to die of heart disease. With four friendships, people benefited most. Why? It's not the number of friends that matters; it's the calibre of the friendship. In building your rope team, don't mistake quantity for quality. You might have hundreds—or even thousands—of "friends" on social media, but how many of those friends would you depend on to lift your spirits, to provide solid life counsel, or to improve your health?

The truth is, in an age when we are supposedly more connected than ever, most of us actually feel like our bonds with our fellow humans are growing weaker. We have fooled ourselves into believing that the quick fix of the social media "like" is enough to get us through the daily struggles. It's only when real challenges pop up in our lives that we realize we don't have the right relationships to help us through. We have lost sight of one of humanity's most precious and crucial resources—*genuine friendship*. And at the core of every rope team is friendship.

An On-Rope friendship is a partnership—two people coming together on equal terms. They give their all for you, and you for them. An On-Rope friendship expects (and endures) the good, the bad, and the ugly and moves both parties forward through adversity and in the direction of each other's Vision.

"I have learned to rely on my Rope Team" is one of the most common statements shared with us after people complete our programs. More than ninety per cent of No Barriers participants agree that "being a part of a team makes me a stronger individual." They start to understand how working with others and being connected with people can make a huge difference as they strive to reach their Vision.

It's human nature to hold your Vision on the inside. It's personal. It's private. It might be scary. If you state it out loud, then you think, "Crap, now I have to do it." It's only when you start sharing your Vision with others on a strong Rope Team that you unleash the full potential of your Vision.

Now, for a deeper understanding of friendship, let's turn to someone who might himself be feeling like an old friend to you at this point in the book.

Grand Philosopher #1
Aristotle

Although the Greek thinker spilled barrels of ink on subjects as varied as physics and ethics and logic, one of his most significant offerings was his ruminations on the power of friendship. In Aristotle's estimation, friendship is perhaps second only to food when it comes to human survival. As he says in *Nicomachean Ethics*:

> Without friends no one would choose to live, though he had all other goods; even rich men and those in possession of office and of dominating power are thought to need friends most of all; for what is the use of such prosperity without the opportunity of beneficence, which is exercised chiefly and in its most laudable form towards friends?

For Aristotle, while we may collect friendships of convenience or advantage over the course of our lives, true and lasting friendships are steeped in virtue. The mark of a strong friendship is reciprocity, a relationship that is mutually beneficial. "To be friends therefore, men must feel goodwill for each other," Aristotle wrote. "That is, wish each other's good, and be aware of each other's goodwill, and the cause of their goodwill must be one of the lovable qualities mentioned above."

In short, true friendship must be a two-way street.

As you take stock of your current friends and consider who might best serve you on your rope team, it's also crucial that you think about who you can serve best. In the strongest of relationships, seeing your friend thrive is as rewarding as thriving yourself.

That said, it is important to note that Aristotle wasn't suggesting we keep the company of friends purely for the sake of our conspicuous usefulness to each other. While good friends can offer a certain utility value to your journey and achieving your Vision, do not discount the deeper value of pleasure, laughter, and shared experiences. These are the threads that will stitch you closer together and make your bond stronger as you help each other along.

In his writings on the subject, Aristotle takes pains to point out that the perfect and virtuous friendship is a rare thing, and we should prepare ourselves for the effort required in developing and nurturing these relationships when we are lucky enough to find them:

> Such friendships are of course rare because such men are few. Moreover, they require time and intimacy . . . People who enter into friendly relations quickly have the wish to be friends, but cannot really be friends without being worthy of friendship, and also knowing each other to be so; the wish to be friends is a quick growth, but friendship is not.

Friendships are vital for our well-being, but they take time to develop and can't be artificially created. You need to be willing to put in the work in order to develop those friendships that will best serve you in your journey.

Grand Philosopher #2
Brené Brown

At the heart of every friendship and rope team is a need for *trust*. Dr. Brené Brown, the five-time *New York Times* best-selling author and a research professor at the University of Houston, has spent the past two decades studying courage, vulnerability, shame, and empathy, and she has an interesting perspective on the concept of trust.

In a 2015 speech that she titled, "The Anatomy of Trust," Brown frames her unique conception of trust in the acronym **BRAVING**, stemming from the idea of how in the process of trusting someone else we are braving a connection with them.

Boundaries. There is no trust between two people without respecting each other's personal boundaries. An important part of those boundaries is being willing to say no.

Reliability. Trust does not exist between friends if one or both of them do not do what they say they will do.

Accountability. It is never easy to apologize or to own up to our mistakes. But if we can't admit our faults and make amends, trust is weakened.

Vault. One of the quickest ways to lose trust in somebody is if they share something with others that you have told them in confidence. Keep a friend's secrets in the vault!

Integrity. Acting from a place of integrity means to choose to do what is right even if it's not easy and comfortable. We earn each other's trust when we act with integrity.

Nonjudgment. Asking for what you need can be hard, and it's only harder if you feel you are being judged when you do. We must offer and receive help without criticism.

Generosity. This really means allowing for mistakes and abiding by the most generous interpretation of a friend's actions or words.

Each of these components come together to form the trust that we need to build strong and impactful friendships. Remembering Brené Brown's acronym will help you as you conduct an audit of your current friendships and determine who among them could best act as a member of your rope team.

ROPE TEAM IN PRACTICE
Dave Shurna and Tom Lillig

Yep, that's us! Within each chapter of this book, we have included profiles of some of our No Barriers participants, showcasing how they have put the Life Elements into action. For Rope Team, we want to tell you the story of our own friendship and how we have become a vital support system for each other. We passionately believe in Rope Team (as well as the other elements) because we have actually put it into practice in our own lives, long before we had given this element a name.

Journey back with us to the seventh grade, when our friendship began on the hardwood of the Emerson Middle School gym. By day, we tried to "Be like Mike" spending hours on the basketball courts dreaming one day we could play a pickup game with Michael Jordan. By night, we cheered on Michael and the Chicago Bulls and suffered with them through their physical struggles against the Pistons before ultimately winning their first of six NBA championships. It has been said that playing basketball with someone reveals their character: *Will they pass to you when you're open? Will they hit the clutch shot when the game is on the line? Will they celebrate with you when you hit it? Will they lift you up when you miss it?* As each of these questions was answered through our games together, the two of us learned to trust each other and to encourage each other. And this formed the basis for our friendship.

During those years, we competed against each other weekly during practice, which fed our competitive flames to beat the other; but when we were in the game, it was all about finding a way together to get the win. During one game, with the score tied and the clock ticking down into the final minutes, our leading scorer found himself in foul trouble. I (Tom) was waved onto the court as a substitute with the game on the line. Dave found me with a pass, and I was immediately fouled, sending me to the free-throw line. There, I netted both foul shots, sealing the win. In that moment, Dave and I proved to be a winning combo.

Although we went to separate high schools, we stayed in touch throughout our high school and college years. Whenever we came together, there were moments that enabled us to build an even stronger connection.

One summer during college, Dave worked a stint at a zoo, and he invited me for a visit. I remember he led me into an enclosure and had me sit still while he approached with a full-grown cheetah. Dave knew that I was terrified of most animals larger than a microwave oven, so seeing the cheetah nearly caused me to pass out. He had the cheetah sit on the ground next to me and encouraged me to pet it. Obviously, I refused. Then he firmly yet calmly pried my shaking hand away from my pants and had me pet the cheetah. I could feel the short, fine hair, the muscular body, and the warmth of an animal I had never dreamed of getting close to, let alone petting. I started to grow comfortable petting the cheetah as I realized her heartbeat was far slower and calmer than mine.

Part of being Dave means that once he pushes past a comfort zone, he must push even further. As I pet the cheetah, Dave said, "Now I want you to touch her tongue." Dave caressed the cheetah's face and convinced her to open her mouth and extend her tongue. My hands immediately retracted and clenched my pants even tighter than the first time. Again, Dave firmly but calmly pried my hand away and encouraged my shaking fingers to touch the cheetah's tongue. He asked me what it felt like. I told him it felt like sandpaper, my voice quivering with fear. Dave then said, "Now I want you to touch her teeth." My response was an immediate "No way." Dave pulled my shaking hand into the mouth of the cheetah. But all of a sudden, the cheetah started slapping her tail hard against the ground. Dave responded by saying in the calmest of voices, "We are going to slowly remove your hand from the cheetah's mouth." We did. To my relief, my shaking hand emerged with all five fingers intact, and the cheetah was able to resume the rest of her day in the enclosure without any dental examinations.

Whether Dave knew it or not at the time, that moment became a testament to our friendship that day, and it helped develop my trust in him.

Later, in January 2002, I was living in Bologna, Italy. Dave had come for a few weeks to visit. After a week of skiing in the Dolomites, Dave became very ill. He could not get any food or liquid down, and while we didn't have a thermometer, I could tell he was burning up. During the middle of the night, he went to the bathroom frequently, but at one point, he simply collapsed to the floor, and I decided he needed to go to the hospital immediately. At 2:00 a.m., with Dave hanging off my arm, I burst into an overcrowded emergency room shouting the only thing that came to mind at that moment, *"C'è un dottore qui? Bisogno di un dottore pronto!"* (Translation: "Is there a doctor here? I need a doctor now!")

Although there were no attending doctors or nurses at the front desk when we entered, other patients who were waiting saw the critical condition Dave was in and came to our aid, echoing my call for immediate assistance more loudly and colourfully. Within two minutes, a team of doctors and nurses dashed out from behind the blocked-off doors and helped me hoist Dave onto a cart. Fearing death was imminent, the pale Dave looked me straight in the eyes and told me a message I should relay to his family. I reassured him that he would be fine and that he was going to make it through. (After all, his doctor's name was Dr. Zucchini. You can't die at the hands of a man named Dr. Zucchini, right?)

With help from an abundance of IV fluids, Dave did, in fact, survive his crazy virus. Even though it may have coloured his visit to Italy, those forty-eight hours in a Bologna hospital grew Dave's trust in me, once again strengthening our friendship.

A few years later, I was back in the United States working for the Peace Corps when Dave reached out about starting an organization, one that would ultimately become the precursor to No Barriers. The vision of the organization resonated deeply with me, and I knew that in some way I needed to be a part of helping Dave get the organization off the ground. I was deeply humbled when I was asked to be the board president of the organization. Dave is a master at building a team, crafting a strategy, and executing the vision. He was the day-to-day driver of the operation and I was excited to be included in his weekly conversations about the direction of the organization. I am forever grateful that Dave invited me to be his strategic co-pilot and always challenged me to bring big, creative ideas that would allow the organization to make an impact on our community.

In December 2009, I received a call from my father while I was on a business trip. My mom had fallen down at work and was being rushed to the hospital. No further details were available, but I knew I needed to cut my trip short and immediately head home. My mom had suffered a massive stroke and died two days later. This woman had been a bright light not just to me and my family but to all who knew her. For her to die suddenly left me feeling unsteady and very much under a dark cloud. I was not a pleasant person to be around and could not access the joy that I had once felt. I was simply numb. Dave was one of several friends from around the country who flew in to support me through this struggle. In the weeks that followed, he knew I was in a depression and pushed for the two of us to go on a trip.

However, a week before the trip, Dave notified me that he and his wife had gone to their twenty-week appointment for their second child, and the doctor informed them that there was no longer a heartbeat. It was a devastating blow for Dave and his wife. Because the child had reached the first trimester, they needed to spend the next day at the hospital to go through the delivery process, which only compounded the emotional suffering. Even in the womb, this child was already so loved by Dave and his wife, and now they had to unexpectedly say goodbye all within a twenty-four-hour period.

Although our suffering was different, our compassion for each other's loss and desire to help in each other's healing was the same. We postponed our trip a few weeks but finally did get an opportunity to escape. We shared stories, we played golf (and lost a lot of balls), we relaxed by a pool. Most importantly, we learned to laugh again.

We made a promise to each other to remember how important it was to be able to reconnect, and since that trip, we have made sure to take an annual trip somewhere in the world every year to both support each other on our respective journeys and to laugh again and again. We're now in the tenth year of our annual adventures, which have taken us to an Ironman competition that concluded at an ancient Roman arena in Croatia, a Lucha Libre wrestling match in Mexico City, an olive oil grove in Sonoma, California, and a bobsled run in Park City, Utah. With each new adventure, the rope that binds us only becomes tighter and more secure.

For me, No Barriers is so much more than just the organization, the curriculum, or this book. It's a shared way forward in a world of continual challenge. After the Ironman race, I started thinking about the concept of No Barriers in running imagery. For me, No Barriers is the reciprocal and never-ending act of wildly cheering each other on as we each struggle and stumble toward our finish lines. My friendship with Dave is a testament to that idea.

BUILDING YOUR ROPE TEAM

Now it's time for you to start recruiting your Rope Team. As you consider who might best fit the roles that we outline below, keep in mind our definition of a Rope Team:

> A group of people who are linked
> together to support a Vision.

It is important to note here that a Rope Team can often be situational. By that, we mean that you might have different On-Rope friends for different parts of your life. We are asking you to look back at your Roadmap and your Vision and think about which On-Rope friends would be most useful for supporting you on the journey.

For example, if you want to get healthy and fit, you might focus on your friends and family who might help you get there. If you want to move into a career that has more meaning, you might look for career mentors. Try to think about your Vision and one particular Reach as you map your Rope Team.

Now, within your Rope Team, there are a variety of roles that team members play for you in your friendship and you for them. Leaning into our climbing metaphor, Rope Teams don't make it up the mountain alone. We have identified the four types of On-Rope friends you want in your life and the distinctive roles that they play as you're moving toward your own Vision.

Type of Friends	Description	Role
Sherpas	The Sherpa people are an ethnic group from Nepal who have lived in the high altitudes of the Himalayas for generations. Their local expertise has been invaluable for foreigners attempting climbs. As we have discussed, in order to achieve our Vision, we need to build strong Rope Teams. It can be scary to share our Vision with others, but we need to embrace the fear and ask for expertise. One part of the Rope Team are the experts who can help navigate the best route to our Vision. These experts, or Sherpas, may be someone you know or someone you need to network to meet. They provide a unique expertise, specific to your Vision, that will assist you as you encounter the inevitable challenges in your way.	Experts
Mountain Guides	While Mountain Guides know about the mountain in front of you, perhaps most importantly, they know you and your unique strengths and weaknesses. Whereas Sherpas are experts in the specific challenge in front of you, Guides, like coaches, know how to pull the right levers to specifically adapt to your needs.	Coach and Mentor

Type of Friends	Description	Role
Climbing Companions	A group of one to four climbers who are linked together by a rope. A strong bond between your Climbing Companions is not only critical to their success, but it's also critical to their survival. Your Climbing Companions understand how important your Vision is to you, and they are there to support you on your journey. They are the people you celebrate and cry with. They are there to remind you why you took this on and that you've got this. These companions play many roles for you. They energize you, comfort you, and challenge you. Without these vital friends, your journey would be far more difficult and far less enjoyable.	Vital Support
Cheer Squad	Your friends, family members, and community at home who are cheering you on. Your Cheer Squad is made up of your loyal friends and family who are cheering you on from afar. While they may not be on the journey with you, they love you and will always be there for you. When you succeed, they are proud of you, and want to share your success with the world. When you fail, they will love you all the same and keep cheering you on toward your next summit.	Emotional Support

Now that you've identified these four types of friends, pull out your Roadmap again and a clean sheet of paper.

Draw four big circles on the page. Write out the names of the four types of friends, one each per circle.

Now, looking at your Roadmap, start filling in the names of all of those friends that you may need on your Rope Team in the circle that's the best fit for them.

Reflect and get comfortable with your list. Remember, if this is *your* Rope Team, you are the Expedition Leader.

Now's the scary part. As the Expedition Leader, we want you to check in with each person or people you have selected to play these roles and ask for their support in achieving your Vision.

We understand that for some people, this may not be an easy task. Asking a person to help you overcome a very personal challenge and achieve your Vision means that you will be trusting them. But don't forget, you have chosen these people for your Rope Team based on their reliability and their trustworthiness, among other qualities. So have faith in yourself that you have made the right decisions, and ask for their support with assuredness.

Building Your Rope Team at Work

The workplace can offer a different dynamic than your personal life when it comes to how you consider your friendships and other relationships. So, we want to briefly walk through some of those variables for those readers whose Vision ties to their work.

In 2012, Google launched Project Aristotle—yes, just like our Grand Philosopher—studying teams across the entire organization to understand and codify the secrets to team effectiveness. Specifically, Google wanted to know why some teams excelled while others fell behind.

Before this study, like many other organizations, Google execs believed that building the best teams meant compiling the best people. It makes sense. The best engineer plus an MBA, throw in a PhD, and there you have it. The perfect team, right? In the words of Julia Rozovsky, Google's people analytics manager, "We were dead wrong."

Instead, here are the traits they found most impactful to a team:

1. **Dependability.** Team members get things done on time and meet expectations.

2. **Structure and clarity.** High-performing teams have clear goals and have well-defined roles within the group.

3. **Meaning.** The work has personal significance to each member.

4. **Impact.** The group believes their work is purposeful and positively impacts the greater good . . . And this last one stood out from the rest.

5. **Psychological Safety.** We've all been in meetings and, due to the fear of seeming incompetent, have held back questions or ideas. It's unnerving to feel

like you're in an environment where everything you do or say is under a microscope. But imagine a different setting—a situation in which everyone is safe to take risks, voice their opinions, and ask judgment-free questions; a culture where managers provide air cover and create safe zones so employees can let down their guard. That's psychological safety.

Both in your personal life and at work, engineering the perfect Rope Team is more subjective than we would like. Ensuring that you have a variety of roles being filled—experts, mentors, peers, and emotional support—as well as evaluating with the five components just listed can and will increase the likelihood that you will build a dream team.

Now let's rejoin Command Sergeant Major Gretchen Evans's story as she puts together her unique Rope Team.

THE DOG THAT PULLED THE ROPE

When Gretchen Evans returned home to the United States after being injured on the battlefield in Afghanistan, she was in need of a Rope Team. She was slipping, and she needed to find those people in her life who would anchor her and help her back to her feet. As she recovered from her trauma, she would need to start building her Rope Team one member at a time.

And, to her relief, that Rope Team would start with Robert.

As Gretchen entered that gymnasium in Fort Sam Houston, the bandage still on her head, her eyes scanned the crowd of waiting family and friends, hoping to find Robert there. At first, she didn't see him. Then, there he was: Robert was standing off to the side, waiting for her, holding a dozen yellow roses. When Gretchen finally reached him, Robert smiled gently and said, "Marry me. Tonight."

Gretchen could barely process how such a thing would be possible. There were so many logistics to handle. But when Robert told her that he had not only secured their Texas marriage license but also pulled a few strings to reserve the chapel right there on base, Gretchen couldn't say no. She changed into her dress blues—which Robert had brought with him—and the two of them married that very night.

For the next two years, the newly married Gretchen stayed at Robert's side as they moved to Italy, where Robert became the chaplain for all of Europe and Southwest Asia. For Gretchen, her time in Italy was like an extended honeymoon. She was happy with Robert. But those two years also proved to be a seemingly healthy way for Gretchen to simply avoid dealing with her trauma. It was only once she moved back to the United States that Gretchen realized there were internal issues that demanded her attention.

In many ways, Gretchen had put a Band-Aid over a festering wound before it had time to heal. When that happens, sometimes a person needs to reopen the wound in order for it to heal properly. With Robert reassigned to a parish stateside, Gretchen began to feel the harm caused by avoiding her problems. She started to wish she had been killed on the battlefield; at least that way, she could have died a hero and been given her last full measure.

Again, she felt like the Scarecrow. As she says in her book, "I had stuffing scattered in Grenada, Nicaragua, Honduras, El Salvador, Panama, Somalia, Kosovo, Iraq, Afghanistan, in my home, on my post, in my church. I was immobilized, defeated, and helpless to help myself. I needed to be put back together, if I had any chance of being whole again. I literally needed to be re-stuffed." In hopes of healing, Gretchen tried everything—medication, meditation, even swimming with sharks. But none of it could put the stuffing back in her.

Instead, the restuffing would take place when Gretchen met another member of her Rope Team: her hearing service dog, Aura.

One day, Gretchen was out for a jog in Decatur, Georgia. She had been running for nearly thirty years, and even though the doctors and specialists warned Gretchen that running could prove dangerous without her hearing, she refused to give it up; she continued to run each morning. That morning, she was jogging on a sidewalk with traffic to her right, when suddenly, a man on a bicycle was riding past her. While he had shouted, "On your left!" Gretchen, of course, hadn't heard him, so she didn't move over. The man accidentally swiped her with his bike, and Gretchen was thrown into the busy road. An oncoming car hit Gretchen, and she was injured pretty badly. She went to the Atlanta VA for medical attention, and there, her team of doctors advised her to either stop running or risk an even worse accident, perhaps fatal.

For Gretchen, this was devastating. She felt like she was at her lowest point. She had already lost so much of her former life. If she gave up running and biking, there would be little left of her that she recognized. So, when she got home from the VA, she scoured the internet for solutions. Finally, she found a potential answer: a service dog. She reached out to America's VetDogs, an organization that helps soldiers find their freedom again. In a short email, she listed her injuries—deafness, PTSD, skeletal issues, traumatic brain injury, morale injury, and other, superficial injuries. Then she simply asked if they could help her.

A response to her email came back almost instantly. It was a single word: "Yes." Only later would Gretchen learn that, in fact, the organization had never before trained a dog for the hearing-impaired. However, the employee on the other end of that email could tell this was Gretchen's cry for help, and there was no way he could say no to her. Instead, he set about to have a dog trained especially for Gretchen. And that dog's name would be Aura.

Aura was able to do many things for Gretchen. She could alert Gretchen to her phone ringing, to a knock at the door, to the microwave beeping. Aura could also fetch Gretchen the TV remote and even turn lights on and off. Perhaps most importantly to Gretchen, Aura could run alongside her as she jogged, alerting Gretchen to any bikers who might be trying to pass her.

As Gretchen puts it, Aura didn't change Gretchen's life, she saved it.

Today, Gretchen Evans is still adding to her Rope Team, which has become invaluable to her in maintaining her Vision for her life. She's also serving on the Rope Teams of other people. To her, Rope Team is a concept that she recognizes from her days in the military, where each soldier looks out for the other soldiers around them. As she says, "When one goes down, you all stop."

Most recently, Gretchen has assembled a team of injured athletes to compete in the *Eco-Challenge*, a televised adventure race that will take place in Fiji. She purposely blended the team with both military vets and civilians to demonstrate the need for these two populations to work together and understand each other. As Gretchen says, the adventure is less about the race and more about awareness and education and, hopefully, change. She has named the team Unbroken.

For Gretchen, Rope Team has become a defining element in her life. It has allowed her to recover from a traumatic experience she once thought she would never come back from. Her Rope Team has also given her the confidence to live her best life.

And, of course, it has put her back on the Yellow Brick Road.

CHAPTER SIX

Summits

"Acknowledging the good that you already have in
your life is the foundation for all abundance."
—*Eckhart Tolle*

TAKE A DEEP BREATH

Vision. Reach. Pioneer. Alchemy. Rope Team. These
are all the tools that we've been defining to
help you crystallize your sense of purpose and
overcome adversities in your life. Together, these
elements form a mindset that will help you create
a future for yourself that does not yet exist.

But there's a problem inherent with the
fearless pursuit of the future: we forget to pause
and appreciate where we are today and how far

we've come. That's important because gratitude gives us energy. And we can learn valuable lessons that help us understand our Vision better and allow us to see where we might need to reach in the future.

For many years at No Barriers, we taught a system of beliefs that was all about understanding who you are and who you want to be. We relied on ancient philosophies, current research, and the life experiences of our tens of thousands of participants to craft the tools you're reading about today. This was our Roadmap to get you to believe that *What's Within You Is Stronger Than What's In Your Way.*

But back in 2015, we realized a critical piece was missing in our school of thought. All this moving forward . . . reaching . . . pioneering . . . stretching to be the best version of ourselves . . . well, *it's exhausting.* And we realized part of what we fail to do as often as we should, as leaders of ourselves and others, is pause. Take a look back at our journey with gratitude. Reflect on the meaning that it had on our lives.

There was a No Barriers expedition team of wounded veterans going up Gannett Peak in Wyoming, and they arrived at an impassable crevasse. This team had been training for months to reach the summit. When they hit this crevasse, they realized they were not going to make it to the top. Suddenly, a cloud of doubt set in. *What had all of this been for? Was it another failed mission? Yet another example of how they couldn't survive and reach goals in their new nonmilitary lives?*

One veteran, Paul Smith, grabbed a stone and said, "This stone represents all the fears I've had about who I'll be in this new body." Ten years earlier, Paul was serving in Iraq when his Humvee triggered an IED and the blast left him burned over fifty per cent of his body. Although his body survived the explosion, his soul suffered greatly. His life back in the United States became a constant struggle with addiction, with depression, with attempts at suicide. But as he stood there at the crevasse, he was able to pause—to reflect—and he realized that he had wasted so much time beating himself up. He was ready to let all that go, to turn his attention to a better future.

Even though Paul and the others weren't going to make it to the summit that day, the epiphany in that moment far outweighed the reward of reaching the top. Paul considered the stone, its symbolic power, and then continued, "I'm ready to let go of that fear." Then Paul tossed the stone in the crevasse. Other veterans did the same, and it became a defining moment of the Summits element for us at No Barriers.

What Paul and the others were able to do was turn a potentially deflating moment into a meaningful moment of gratitude. They were able to see their current struggle within the greater context of their journey by taking a deep breath and reflecting on how they had reached that moment. In doing so, they could be grateful for all that had come before it.

DEFINING SUMMITS

Summits is the process of reflecting back on your experiences with gratitude for the gifts of learning. It's reflecting on the struggle and finding meaning in the journey while also being grateful for all the people who have helped you reach this particular moment. Sitting with your journey and recognizing how far you have come, that is the key to Summits.

If you've ever been to the summit of a mountain, you know the feeling of being on top of the world looking out at all the other peaks and valleys. You can literally see the path that got you to the top. You can imagine (and sometimes see) the many peaks you climbed along the way that got you to that point.

But you'll notice that in naming this element, we didn't frame it as a singular summit. That is because there is not just one summit for you to consider as you climb. Having a limited definition of a summit—seeing it only as the very top of that mountain—can often cause us to miss the smaller summits along the way. When you are climbing the metaphorical mountains of your journey, sometimes you can be so focused on the peak—relentlessly driving toward that end point you have envisioned—that you miss a more meaningful lesson, experience, or perspective that your journey has to offer you.

So, we want you to take a moment—right now— to look back over your shoulder and see the view from here.

That's right. We want you to put this book down and find a quiet space. Take the next five minutes to reflect with gratitude.

We ask you to think of ONE thing from the book—it can be anything—for which you are grateful. Write it down.

Acknowledge your effort so far. Acknowledge what you have learned. Far too often, we crank through our activities without pausing. Let this be your time to allow yourself to sit with gratitude.

WHY SUMMITS MATTER

You know those moments when you've got your head down and you're powering through a task or project? It's that stretch of time—be it a day or a week or even several months—where you feel like you have a rhythm going, and you are singularly focused on exactly what you set out to do. You're in the zone. During that time, you allow yourself to embrace a routine, which makes you feel productive and efficient.

But sometimes this means you have slipped into autopilot mode. And even though you might feel like you are accomplishing what you set out to do, it's possible that you are missing the bigger picture. When you allow yourself to go into autopilot, your mind is often simply storing up knowledge and experiences without actually taking the time necessary to process it all. Summits is about reclaiming agency over your actions and intentions by taking the requisite time to reflect and to be grateful for what has brought you to this point.

The Value of Reflection

At its core, reflection is deliberative contemplation. It is a way to pause and organize your collected knowledge and experiences in order to process their full significance. Often, people accomplish this through mindfulness, or meditation, or even prayer.

John Dewey, one of America's preeminent philosophers in the first half of the twentieth century, focused intensely on the importance of reflection and how the act of reflecting can help us solve the problems before us.

As he writes in his book *How We Think*:

> As long as our activity glides smoothly along from one thing to another, or as long as we permit our imagination to entertain fancies at pleasure, there is no call for reflection. Difficulty or obstruction in the way of reaching a belief brings us, however, to a pause. In the suspense of uncertainty, we metaphorically climb a tree; we try to find some standpoint from which we may survey additional facts.

When Dewey talks about those moments when "our activity glides smoothly," he is referring to those times when we go into autopilot. It's only when something gets in our way, when we are forced to stop and think, that we attempt to view the situation from a new vantage and gain additional facts and ideas to help us break through.

But here's the problem we now face nearly a hundred years after Dewey opined on the importance of reflection: the twenty-first century has made it increasingly difficult for us to stop and think, to shake ourselves out of autopilot.

Right now, we're living through a time of cognitive and sensory overload. Just think about how much your phone alone hijacks your attention throughout the day as each new push notification sends you to your email, to social media, to Slack messages from colleagues that you receive outside of business hours. Every app in your phone and every streaming platform on your television has been insidiously designed with a singular mandate: to control your attention as long as possible. Whether we like to admit it or not, we are participants in an attention economy that demands a tight grip on every last thing our mind focuses on. And this makes the act of reflection a far greater challenge than it was even ten or twenty years ago.

The science of the mind tells us that our *attentional space* is limited. There are only so many things your mind will allow you to process at once. By giving your attention to one thing, it means you are pulling it from another. Whether we know it or not, there is always a cost when we allow our attention to be lured away by the dopamine drip of social media or the sometimes false sense of productivity we get by keeping our minds thinking about work even when we're not truly accomplishing anything.

By recognizing that cost, you can better assess what things you should pay less attention to in order to reserve more space for deeper reflection.

In Summits, we want to help you to condition your brain to thoughtfully reflect. By practicing mindfulness and other attentional training techniques, you will be able to replace stimulus-driven attention with a more self-directed attention. In doing so, you will become more reflective, allowing you to gain a fuller perspective on the lessons of your journey.

The Value of Gratitude

Another key component of Summits is cultivating gratitude. Frequently, when you are focused only on what's ahead, you tend to dwell on those things you don't yet have, and you lose sight of the things you already do have. Gratitude is the act of appreciating those people, relationships, and achievements already in your life.

So why is it important to be grateful and to appreciate what you already have? Because gratitude gives you energy—it provides the fuel for your journey ahead. There is an insightful children's book by Carol McCloud titled, *Have You Filled a Bucket Today?* and it serves as a guide to happiness for kids. But it is equally as instructive for adults. The general concept of the book is that all of us carry around an invisible bucket. Our level of happiness (or lack thereof) depends on how full that bucket is. To fill the bucket, we engage in positive thinking, gratitude, and acts of kindness. With a full bucket, we have energy for daily life. When we neglect our invisible buckets and allow them to go empty, we become enervated and depressed.

Dr. Robert Emmons, a renowned psychologist who studies the science of gratitude and its effects on well-being, supports the notion that gratitude can fuel a person's optimism, ambitions, and even physical health. In his book *Gratitude Works!* Emmons describes different ways that you can cultivate gratitude in your own life. As he says, "Living gratefully begins with affirming the good and recognizing its sources. It is the understanding that life owes me nothing and all the good I have is a gift, accompanied by an awareness that nothing can be taken for granted."

He outlines not only some more obvious methods, such as expressing your thanks to people around you who have helped you in some way, but he also delves into more internal and personal ways to nurture gratitude, such as keeping a daily *gratitude journal* that will remind you of the goodness that is present in your life.

We will detail a few more of Emmons's exercises a little later in the how-to section of this chapter, but the key takeaways here are the benefits that gratitude can have on your health and attitude, which will both be critical in your efforts to overcome adversity. Our main goal at No Barriers is not simply for you to find your purpose and overcome your particular adversity—it's to accomplish those things *while* remaining healthy, both mentally and physically. If you are not taking the time to cultivate gratitude, you are likely depriving your mind and body of the fuel they need on this journey.

You may be saying to yourself, how is it that I can practice gratitude when things don't seem very positive right now? When terrible things happen, what can you be grateful for? At No Barriers, we have worked with people who have suffered through tremendous physical and mental trauma. In no way do we expect people to be grateful for the accident that took their leg, or the cancer that took the life of a parent, or the discrimination that took a person's job. Rather, we ask them to examine a wider range of their experiences and see if there are areas of gratitude within this broader context. We don't expect a person to be grateful for the accident, but they might have experienced gratitude from the love they felt from their family throughout the ordeal. Or the gratitude for knowing the parent's love even if that parent has passed. Throughout our lives, we believe it's important to reflect and look for those moments of gratitude, most especially when they are hard to find.

SUMMITS IN PRACTICE

The very moment Kyle Maynard came into this world, the nurses rushed him out of the delivery room before his parents could even get a glimpse of their firstborn child. The doctor had unspoken concerns with the health of Kyle and needed to check on a few things before the Maynards could meet their new son. The minutes that would elapse before they finally saw their son would be the longest of their lives. When they finally got to meet Kyle, the Maynards saw why the doctor had been so concerned—his legs ended at his knees, and his arms ended at his elbows. The doctor told them their son had a rare disorder known as congenital amputation.

Kyle's parents were shocked. Not one of the diagnostic tests administered during the pregnancy indicated that their son would be born with a disability. They hadn't prepared themselves for the challenges that such a disability presented, and they hadn't considered the accommodations they might need to make for Kyle. They were suddenly asking themselves questions they never thought they would need answers to: *How would he learn to feed himself? Would their son ever become self-sufficient? How was Kyle going to get around in a world that wasn't built for people like him?*

For Kyle's father, his instinct was to help Kyle adapt to the world, rather than hope the world would adapt to him. This approach proved to make all the difference in Kyle's life. Together, Kyle and his dad worked at inventing ways for Kyle to put on his clothes by himself, to use a fork and spoon at the dinner table, and even to ride a homemade bike. For each new challenge that the world presented, Kyle learned how to pioneer his way around, over, or through that problem.

By the time Kyle was approaching his teen years, he was constantly seeking out opportunities to prove that his body was not as limiting as people thought. When he told his parents he wanted to play for the local football team, his mother was reluctant at first. However, Kyle ultimately convinced her to let him try out.

Kyle made the team. Although he wasn't in the starting line-up, his coach gave him plenty of time out on the field to prove his worth as a nose tackle. As Kyle says of his tenure on the football team, "I didn't quit or give up. I met the adversity with a full head of steam. I wanted to change the way players and coaches saw me—not as a disabled player but as a defensive lineman who could inflict more damage than anyone else had before."

Kyle enjoyed football. It gave him a fuller sense of himself, and he thrived on the feeling of being part of a team. After his first season on the gridiron, he decided to join the wrestling team, mainly to keep in shape for the next football season. But when Kyle got out on the mat, he realized what a good fit the sport was for him. He was able to use his body strategically to bring down his opponents. And while he racked up over thirty consecutive losses in his first season (and zero wins), he refused to give up.

As Kyle got into high school, he realized that his unique body type offered a psychological advantage against his opponent—and that's when he began to win. Together, he and his coach developed signature moves that only Kyle was capable of, and Kyle started to see consistent results on the mat. Over the course of his high school wrestling career, Kyle went 35–16, winning far more than he lost.

Throughout his childhood and teenage years, Kyle embraced a simple, two-word motto: *No excuses*. To him, every excuse you make keeps you away from the things you most want out of life. This motto allowed him to see around the corners of his perceived limitations and do more with his body than most people thought possible. (The motto also became the title of his memoir, which he wrote and published while attending college.)

As Kyle succeeded on the mat, he looked for other ways to put his motto into practice. He turned to weightlifting, where he earned GNC's title of the World's Strongest Teen by doing twenty-three repetitions of 240 pounds on the bench press. Shortly after that, in 2004, Kyle was named Best Athlete with a Disability by ESPN. This led to interviews with Oprah Winfrey and *Larry King Live*.

For Kyle, each new seemingly impossible challenge he overcame gave him the sensation one gets from drinking seawater—every sip he took only made him thirstier. He had to have more. So, in 2012, Kyle set his sights on an actual summit: Mount Kilimanjaro.

At twenty-five, Kyle travelled to Tanzania, where he would attempt to climb the dormant volcano that rises 19,431 feet into the clouds. As he looked at the mountain in front of him, he likely thought back to all the times he had to pioneer his way through a world not tailored to his disability. This journey would demand everything of him. He would have to hike thirty-eight miles on the mountain, bear-crawling on all fours the entire way. To protect himself from the rough terrain, he had to wear specialized boots on his arms and legs.

Along with a team of climbers, Kyle began the projected ten-day journey with optimism. He proved to be adept at climbing, and going upward actually took the pressure off his arms. However, it was when Kyle and the team had to hike down a slope or across flat portions that Kyle's body began to suffer. Even though Kyle was used to pushing himself to the brink, by day five of the journey, his body and his willpower were reaching a breaking point.

That's when his team's guide came to him with a plan B: they could just climb straight up to the summit, rather than hiking the trail. While this option would take the pressure off his arms, it also offered its own risks, such as loose rocks and avalanches, and there were no guarantees that they would make it to the top. Kyle, knowing his arms wouldn't make it if they took the longer, flatter route, opted for the more dangerous path upward.

By the ninth day, Kyle and the team were wiped. He looked up at the summit and felt like it was still too far away. "The most frustrated I got the whole day was when I'd go and look up and see how far I had to go."

Kyle was making the mistake that most of us make: we forget to appreciate the distance we've already travelled and focus only on the distance ahead. But as the end of the ninth day approached, Kyle finally took the time to turn around and look back down the mountain. He turned that moment of exhaustion and frustration into a moment of reflection and gratitude. That small but focused action gave Kyle the fuel he needed to make it the rest of the way.

When Kyle reached the top of Mount Kilimanjaro, he became the first quadruple amputee to manage such a feat. This accomplishment earned him a second awarding of the title Best Male Athlete with a Disability by ESPN. But for Kyle, the real reward of that particular climb was the new perspective on pushing through his most challenging moments. Oftentimes, it's just as important to take the time to sit and go on an inward journey—dedicating a moment to sit back and take it in, where the journey has led and where it's going.

A HOW-TO FOR SUMMITS

The key to Summits is finding the space for *reflection* and *gratitude*. But it's harder than it sounds. So often in our lives today, we feel the pressure to always be moving, which leaves us mistaking activity for meaningful progress. You run and run and run, moving through your days thinking you're getting closer to your destination; however, when you finally take the time to look down, you realize that you're on a treadmill.

And here's the thing about a treadmill: you can run as fast as you want, but you're not actually moving forward. To avoid making this mistake, you need to find ways to clear the distractions and meaningless activities in your routine.

Here are a few suggestions:

No-Technology Sundays. We are so distracted by the constant array of information that is either piped through our phones or our computers or our televisions. Texts, push notifications, social media check-ins, and the tyranny of our email inboxes can be a constant tug on our attention.

For just one day a week, engage in a *digital detox*. Turn it all off every Sunday. Just see what happens when you turn off distraction for a full twenty-four hours. We find it leads naturally to moments of reflection and introspection.

The Gratitude Journal. Each day, carve out a few minutes to jot down the things you are grateful for. Try to find the joy or satisfaction derived from even the smallest and most ordinary moments. Think about the people who have helped you throughout the day, whether it is a colleague or a teacher at your child's school.

In his research, Robert Emmons has found that keeping a gratitude journal—even just once a week—promotes a healthier lifestyle. Those people who keep the journal are more likely to exercise, and they are more optimistic about the day or week ahead.

Attentional Training. Philosopher and psychologist, William James, once said, "My experience is what I agree to pay attention to." Think about that: everything that you give your attention to throughout the day is influencing how you experience this life. Don't you think it's time to become more aware of what is occupying your attention?

Training your attention is about recognizing what stimuli are pulling at your mind. Find a time in the evening to spend just a few minutes—no longer than the time it takes to brush your teeth—to reflect on what occupied your attention throughout the day. If a greater portion of your attention was stimulus-driven, make an effort the next day to self-direct your attention, ensuring that you have more agency over what you focus on. Remember, choosing what to give your attention to also means you are choosing what not to give your attention to. What is missing from your life experience because you are not taking control of your attention?

The Lessons Learned Cairn. Go outside and collect about ten rocks. Reflect on your journey so far and identify the turning points or milestones. Write one milestone on each rock. Then write one thing you are grateful you learned from that milestone. Build all your rocks into a small tower, or cairn, and put the cairn in a prominent location that you see every day. Let it serve as a reminder of the gifts of your journey. Don't like to build things? Do the same activity but in a journal.

Great Big Ball of Hope Meditation. There's a Buddhist meditation that focuses on hope. You start to picture individual people or individual events in your life that have been part of your journey. When one comes to mind, you sit with it and try to imagine all the reasons you should have hope because that individual exists or that event happened. Sit with it and think hopefully about it for as long as it lasts. Then move on to the next person/event. Imagine you're building a ball of hope.

Write a Thank-You Letter. Sit down right now and think of one person who has helped you on your journey. It could be a family member, it could be a public figure who has inspired you, it could be a colleague. Write a letter to him or her about why you're thankful for him or her. Better yet, call the person. Let them really feel how thankful you are.

You may have noticed that this chapter is structured a little differently than all the others. That's intentional. Oftentimes, we can find ourselves being lulled by a consistent rhythm or pattern, and this can make us miss the critical moments of reflection. With Summits, we want you to stop and take the time needed to consider how you have reached this point in your journey and to be grateful for the people or events that have helped you get here.

In our programs, here's what more than eighty-five per cent of our participants say they've learned about Summits: "I can identify specific things that I have learned from my experiences" and "I reflect on my experiences in order to grow." As one teacher shared, "The program helped me learn the power of reflection and how to create situations where reflection is encouraged." In Summits, participants learn how important it is to pause, take a breath, and appreciate the journey.

Now, remember at the start of this chapter when we asked you to put the book down and write down one key thing you have learned from this book so far. Take that piece of paper back out, read what you wrote, and allow your gratitude for that thing to be your fuel as you head into our last Life Element, *Elevate*.

CHAPTER SEVEN

Elevate

"The sole meaning of life is to serve humanity."
—Leo Tolstoy

LIVING THE LIFE YOU WANT RIGHT NOW

Something good is going to happen. This was the inscription on a necklace that Whitney Way Thore's mother had gifted her in November 2013. It was meant to encourage the thirty-year-old Whitney, to give her a much-needed morale boost. But Whitney wasn't in the right mindset to receive such a hopeful sentiment, and her glib reaction was, "Okay, but when?"

For years, Whitney had been caught in the undertow of self-doubt and depression brought on by body image issues. From a young age, she was always just slightly bigger than the other girls around her—in dance class, on the soccer team, in her theatre troupe. When she took the lead as Dorothy in the fifth-grade musical, Whitney knew she stood out from the other girls around her: not just because she had a natural talent as a dancer and performer, but also because she was larger, both in height and weight. Most girls at this age begin comparing their bodies to other girls around them, and Whitney was no exception. These comparisons became a source of anxiety for Whitney, and the notion that she was not like everyone else would have a lasting impact on her sense of self-worth. To her, at that tender age, it didn't matter if she thought she was pretty; it only mattered what those around her thought.

As Whitney moved through middle school, her body image issues deepened. While she gained popularity among her classmates, there were always those kids who instinctively knew her Achilles' heel: fat shaming. They would crack jokes about her thicker thighs or her larger backside; some even took to calling her Baby Beluga. By the seventh grade, Whitney began to mark her calendar with "ND" and "NL"—"No Dinner" and "No Lunch"—making sure to skip at least one meal each day. For Christmas that year, she asked for exercise equipment. And when skipping meals and working out didn't seem to have the effect on her waistline that she desired, she turned to a more drastic measure. Whitney would retreat to the bathroom after meals and force herself to throw up by sticking the handle of a toothbrush down her throat.

By the time Whitney was a junior in high school, she was weighing herself daily, stepping onto a scale when she woke up in the morning to see if she had shed any weight the day before. Her body image was now on her mind most hours of the day—literally from the moment she got out of bed—and not only because of the cruel comments she endured from some kids at school. At home, there was a steady undercurrent of offhand remarks from her parents about her weight. Whenever her mother would snap photos of Whitney, she would casually instruct Whitney to suck in her stomach. And her father would often admonish her not to eat anything "extra" after meals, subtly policing what Whitney ate. (Today, so many years later, Whitney acknowledges that even though her parents loved her deeply and were well-intentioned, they were misguided about weight loss, just as most of us are.)

With the combination of the unspoken pressure from her parents to lose weight and the social pressure to be thin like other girls in her dance class, Whitney redoubled her efforts. At the recommendation of her father, she began seeing a nutritionist who outlined a healthy diet for her. For the most part, she stuck to the recommended diet, although she continued purging after meals. She also added a new component to her routine. She would take Adderall, which proved to be an appetite suppressant. With all of these elements combined, Whitney managed to lose thirty pounds in three months, making her the smallest she had been in high school at 130 pounds. Of course, the routine was far from healthy, both physically and psychologically, but Whitney was desperate for the approval of her parents and her peers.

In her senior year, Whitney continued to dance and perform in community theatre, and she thrived both academically and socially. At her senior prom, Whitney was crowned prom princess (just after she secretly purged her dinner in the gym bathroom). Then, after she graduated from high school, she set her sights on college, hoping she could leave the anxiety about her weight behind her.

But that was not to be. As Whitney recounts in her 2016 memoir, *I Do It with the Lights On*, just before her parents drove her to college in the fall, her dad found a private moment in the car to say to Whitney, "There are a couple of things I wish we'd had some more progress with before you went off to school. I wish I'd introduced you more to religion, and I wish you'd lost some more weight. But there's plenty of time for those two things, so no big deal."

Again, although Whitney's father thought he was speaking out of compassion for his daughter, his words were misguided and only reinforced the negative social pressures around body image. In her book, Whitney muses on this moment with her father: "I wonder now, fourteen years later, if my dad could have imagined that I still wouldn't have made the progress we wanted with weight loss, that it *is* a big deal, and that as a thirty-two-year-old woman, I'd be writing a book about why."

Whitney's struggle with her weight only worsened in college. In her first semester away at school, the weight gain felt relentless. Her jeans got tighter on her waist, and her stomach felt pudgier than any other time in her life. Instead of the "Freshman 15" that college students often put on in their first semester, Whitney says she gained the "Freshman 50." Socially, she retreated to her bedroom, self-conscious about her body. Academically, her grades suffered as she attended class less and less, a black cloud of depression keeping her in bed. (Perhaps most alarming to Whitney was the F she received in her dance class, the one part of her identity about which she was still passionate.)

By the time Whitney went home for summer break, she was weighing in at 200 pounds. Although she spent the summer months working out and vigilantly monitoring her diet, she returned to campus in the fall thirty pounds heavier than when she left. No matter what Whitney did, the stubborn weight gain would not subside. She felt more helpless and hopeless than at any other time in her life.

Then, a bittersweet revelation: when she visited her OB-GYN, a nurse practitioner told Whitney that she might have a disorder known as polycystic ovary syndrome (PCOS). The syndrome is marked by severe weight gain, irregular periods, and thinning hair—all symptoms that Whitney was experiencing. Upon further testing, Whitney was officially diagnosed with PCOS. Although this brought a certain amount of distress because she now had to confront the realities of the illness, there was also a sense of relief that stemmed from a fuller understanding of her unique body.

In some ways, the news of PCOS freed her of the shame she had internalized for so long—the years of anxiety prompted by weight gain. Her body's inability to properly distribute insulin had a direct relationship with her inability to keep the weight off. And this realization prompted Whitney to call up her father and reveal to him the impact of not just *his* words about her weight but also the words of her mother and her friends, and society at large. Over the years, she had unconsciously assimilated the offhand comments, the diet policing, the magazine covers featuring only thin girls, the never-ending ads for weight-loss programs; and now it was all coming to the surface. As she considers in her book:

> One, or even some, of these things might not have derailed the self-worth that I'd like to believe is innate in human beings. But all of these things, coming at me from every direction, had broken down a talented dancer, a soccer champion, a prom princess. They left this twenty-two-year-old woman feeling like a lost child, desperately searching for any kind of assurance that her life was not completely over when she felt with every fibre of her being that it was.

Whitney finished college strong, rededicating herself to her studies and to the theatre. After graduation, Whitney braved a new adventure, traveling to South Korea, where she took a job teaching English to Korean students. Although she found the job rewarding, Whitney was shocked by how openly the culture fat-shamed her. There are fewer overweight people in South Korea, so Whitney stuck out even more than back at home. Everyone from taxi drivers to store clerks to her students would carelessly remark about her weight. She even became accustomed to jeers and insults about her body when walking the streets.

While she continued to diet and work out sporadically in South Korea, overall, her body weight maintained its upward trend. And by the end of her stint in the country, Whitney was tipping the scales at over 300 pounds. Determined to fix her body, Whitney—now nearing thirty—moved home with her parents and pledged to lose some of the weight, no matter how impossible that mission felt.

With the encouragement of her parents and the help of a trainer, Whitney established a gruelling workout routine and a strict diet that she stuck to for an entire year. As she says, losing weight became her singular obsession, and over the course of that year, Whitney managed to lose 100 pounds.

But while it felt like an accomplishment to trim her waistline, it came with a cost. She had no time for anything else. Whitney had to fight endlessly to keep off each pound she lost; and at some point, centring her whole life on weight loss became impractical. As she let up on her rigorous training schedule in order to make more time for work and relationships, the scale began to count up once again. It wasn't long before Whitney had not only gained back the hundred pounds she had lost, but she added an extra thirty to that number. Whitney's hope of ever losing weight in a meaningful way had disappeared. The unavoidable truth was that the odds were stacked against her in this endeavour. Once again, the cloud of depression set in.

It was in that low moment that Whitney's mother had given her that necklace, the one with the inscription: *Something good is going to happen.*

While, at first, Whitney didn't think she was in a place to hear that message of hope from her mother, it turns out there was a deeper meaning to be gleaned in those words. Whitney woke up to the fact that she was always looking to the future for something good to happen. She was constantly thinking about what life *would* be like when she reached her target weight. In a way, she forever saw her body as "in transition," not where it should be yet.

That's when Whitney realized she had to adopt a new perspective, one that emphasized the present:

Live the life you want right now.

It was around the time of this epiphany that Whitney was offered a free boudoir photo shoot from a local portrait photographer. Whitney's immediate instinct was to turn it down. She was now at 340 pounds, the heaviest she had ever been. But a key promise she had made to herself with this new approach to life was to embrace things outside her comfort zone. As she says, "Instead of declining an opportunity on the basis of my body insecurity, I would force myself to take it anyway."

So, after stuffing her insecurities away, Whitney sat for the boudoir shoot . . . and for the first time in decades, she didn't cringe at a photo of herself. Her reaction was quite the opposite: as she looked through the images of herself, she thought they were the sexiest photos anyone had ever taken of her. And it was all because she was determined to change her perspective.

But while Whitney had been able to finally change the way she saw herself, changing other people's attitudes about body image would prove a far greater challenge. In an act that would be both liberating and terrifying at once, Whitney posted the photos of her from the boudoir shoot to social media; and the responses came fast and furious. While there were plenty of "You go, girl!" sentiments from friends, there was also a host of outspoken detractors. The most common critique was that Whitney was promoting obesity by posting the pictures. The nastier comments indicated that Whitney should be ashamed of her body.

Perhaps the comment that cut deepest was from her own father, who privately told Whitney he found the photos unflattering. He tearfully said to Whitney, "I want people to respect you and not have their view of you clouded by the fact that you're fat." As her father, he wanted so much for his daughter, and he knew she had the heart and mind to do good in the world. But until she lost the weight, he was afraid people wouldn't be able to accept her.

Instead of shrinking away from her father's comments, Whitney doubled down on her promise to stop caring what other people thought about her body and start living in it. She printed up pages and pages of comments from hundreds of women who not only sympathized with Whitney but also praised her for her courage. Many of the women, whether overweight or not, had first-hand experience with body image issues, and they were grateful that someone was willing to be vulnerable and open about the very real struggle. Whitney gave those pages to her father and told him he was making the same mistake as everyone else. Society wanted women's bodies to be ornaments, when, in fact, they should be instruments.

Whitney's interactions on social media—both positive and negative—only encouraged her to put herself out there more. The more she learned that other women felt exactly the way she felt, she wanted to reach out to them and reassure them that it was okay—they didn't have to feel ashamed of their bodies. They didn't have to feel like they were constantly in transition. They no longer had to give in to their insecurities. *They could live the life they wanted right now.*

For Whitney personally, she realized her own insecurities had caused her to give up what she was most passionate about—dancing—and she was determined to correct this. With the help of her childhood friend Todd, Whitney choreographed a dance to the song "Talk

Dirty" by Jason Derulo. Then they filmed it. The video showcased Whitney in all her confident glory, unafraid and unashamed, but deep down, she knew this was the most vulnerable she had ever allowed herself to get. She titled the video "A Fat Girl Dancing." When she and Todd discussed posting the video on YouTube, she was both excited and anxious. She was definitely putting herself out there for all to see (and critique).

Then Whitney posted the video, and she waited to see how the world would react . . .

DEFINING ELEVATE

For the majority of this book, we've had you thinking about *your* Vision, *your* Reach, *your* Rope Team. But along the way—through the stories we've shared—we've been alluding to a critical concept, one that is a guiding force through your journey and is directly tied to the strength of your Vision. That concept is Elevate.

For centuries, some of our greatest thinkers have come to the same conclusion: true happiness is found in helping others. Consider the words of Mahatma Gandhi: "The best way to find yourself is to lose yourself in the service of others." To fully unleash your own potential, you need to create a Vision for yourself that is about much more than just you, a Vision that also lifts up those around you.

Elevate means that you positively impact the world as a leader who serves others. It requires shifting your lens from an internal focus to an external one. Elevate is the moment that you go from a *me* to a *we*. As you do so, you start to think about how you as a leader can be a vehicle to make others better and to make the world a better place.

Throughout the other chapters leading up to this one, you've seen the concept of Elevate already in action, even if we didn't name it specifically. When Erik Weihenmayer was told not to let Everest be his greatest accomplishment and he then unleashed a much greater potential in himself and others by inspiring the No Barriers movement—that was Elevate. Remember when Mandy Harvey reached nearly half a billion viewers on YouTube when her Golden Buzzer moment on *America's Got Talent* went viral? Instead of making that moment just about her, Mandy realized that she could use her new platform to stoke a fire in others, to teach them how to overcome their own obstacles. There again, you saw Elevate. The same goes for Hugh Herr as he established the biomechatronics lab at MIT, developing prosthetic technologies that would help so many people beyond just himself. Or J.R. Martinez, who used his comeback story to show people that recovery is possible even after the worst of traumas; or Gretchen Evans, who gave hope to the thousands of wounded vets struggling with PTSD just like her.

Do you see the connection here? Each of the people we profiled became leaders who gained strength from thinking of the impact they could have on others and the world. When you talk to each of them now, they get far greater joy and fulfilment by watching others flourish—by seeing the impact of their work on the lives of real people.

Yes, their Visions started out as a focus on themselves, but they evolved into something so much more.

The principle of Elevate is rooted in the idea that when we make our Vision about much more than ourselves, not only do we receive much more fulfilment for ourselves, but we also unleash great power in others. And the collective impact is extraordinary. When you start to look outside yourself and your own growth and think about how you can Elevate others around you, your community, and the world, the light inside of you that was stoked with your Vision erupts into a raging wildfire.

WHY ELEVATE MATTERS

Through Whitney Way Thore's story, we can learn why Elevate is so important. Initially, Whitney saw her struggle through a single lens focused on her. She felt isolated and helpless in her perennial battle with her weight and size, and that often caused her to retreat from the world even further.

But as Whitney came to realize that she was not alone in her struggle with body image issues and that other people needed the same help she sought, she took heart and hope in knowing that hers was a shared struggle. By showing others it was okay to live without shame, Whitney was able to develop her own source of confidence. Elevate paid dividends not just to others but to herself as well.

Other times, Elevate is important because the situation requires it. When there's an emergency or tragedy, we are all called to step up and help each other in whatever way we can. Fred Rogers (someone who we will profile later in this chapter) reminds us to "look for the helpers," to remain optimistic in the face of crisis. For those of us who are in the middle of it, we are often called to BE the helpers and Elevate those around us who are most in need.

Throughout the COVID-19 pandemic, there have been numerous helpers who have stepped up in extraordinary ways to assist those in need. One such helper is Dr. Rana Awdish in Detroit. Dr. Awdish is a critical care physician and the medical director for the Henry Ford Hospital's care experience program, where she takes very seriously the ways in which she can show empathy for both the patients and the physicians.

In March 2020, as the surge in patients hit the hospital, Dr. Awdish made a point to visit each of the twelve units treating COVID-19 patients, talking with the doctors, nurses, and other members of the team about how they were holding up. With each unit treating eight to sixteen patients, she knew that they would be dealing with both physical and emotional exhaustion. She wanted to be present to their needs and make sure their worries and concerns were getting heard.

Another primary concern was obviously her patients and, in particular, their ability to stay connected with their families. For safety reasons, the hospital enforced strict visitor restrictions that forced patients to suffer without family members nearby. Dr. Awdish secured 300 iPads and iPhones. With these devices, sick patients could now video chat with their loved ones in a more intimate way, "eye to eye," as Dr. Awdish says.

Our favourite tradition that Dr. Awdish and her colleagues launched during the pandemic was the playing of Journey's "Don't Stop Believing" through the hospital sound system every time a COVID-19 patient was discharged. The song gave the entire hospital a chance to feel joy, hope, and solidarity, and an opportunity to reflect (and belt out) with gratitude.

As Elevate relates to our No Barriers programs, more than ninety-six per cent of our participants leave our programs believing that they have a "responsibility to contribute to something bigger than myself" and that they "want to make a difference." We have countless versions of a statement like this from our program participants: "The program not only taught me about myself but that I have a responsibility and ability to have a positive impact on the world."

This data point is so important to pause and reflect upon. First and foremost, we're arming people with a philosophy that will compel them to go out in the world and make a positive difference. Second and just as important, think back to the story of Frankl and the concentration camp. The fuel that empowers us to break through adversity requires a Vision that Elevates others and the world. You'll ignite that fire in this chapter.

The truth is, we often forget how universal the human experience is. The things we are feeling and enduring are likely the same things our neighbours and colleagues are feeling and enduring as well. And once we can acknowledge this—once we can allow our personal journeys to evolve into a collective journey—we start to reap rewards we might not have expected.

Here are just a few ways that Elevate matters to both you and others:

The World Needs You. Giving to others often has a cascading effect: you give to one person, that person then feels compelled to pass on a good deed to someone else, and so on. The result can be stronger social connections and greater morale in your community. You and everyone around you will benefit, likely boosting the overall sense of happiness and well-being. As the saying goes, *A rising tide lifts all boats.*

But, of course, the opposite is true as well. If you disengage from your community and neglect to give, to volunteer, to work to build up other people, the cascade effect will be damaging and the sense of community will contract.

This is evidenced most clearly in our current moment. As a report released by the University of Maryland's Do Good Institute shows, the national volunteer rate in the United States has dropped nearly thirty per cent within a decade. During that time, the country also saw a decline in giving to nonprofits. The director of the Do Good Institute, Robert Grimm, cautions about this trend's lasting consequences: "Continued declines in community participation will produce detrimental effects for everyone, including greater social isolation, less trust in each other, and poor physical and mental health."

Right now, we are seeing people around the United States and the globe retreating into their own corners, more reluctant than ever to give, and becoming less willing to join together to address big issues such as climate change and poverty.

So, what can you do? When you connect your Vision to a bigger cause, you channel your purpose into something greater for the world. It doesn't mean you have to go out and be Mother Teresa. But when you shift the lens from yourself to others, your Vision starts to have ripple effects that can change the world.

It Empowers Others to Grow. Great leaders Elevate others. Author Liz Wiseman calls these great leaders "Multipliers" and says that "Multipliers are genius makers. Everyone around them gets smarter and more capable." When we learn to Elevate others, we get better results. These are the kinds of teams everyone wants to be a part of.

It's Good for You. Think back on the last time you performed a good deed for someone else. It could be a gesture as small as holding the door open for another person as you left the grocery store, or an act of paying it forward when you went through the drive-through at a Starbuck's and picked up the tab for the car behind you. Do you remember how you felt after performing that good deed? More than likely, it gave you a warm, positive sensation. It felt good for your soul, right?

But here's the thing: it's not just good for your soul, but it's also good for your heart, your lungs, your general health, and well-being. Reams of recent research show that giving to others around you, and even to the wider community, can actually be a boon to your health, both physically and mentally.

Consider one study conducted by Doug Oman at the University of California, Berkeley. His findings showed that elderly people who volunteered for two or more organizations increased their chances of a longer life. In fact, they were forty-four per cent less likely to die over a five-year period than those who did not volunteer. As another study by Claremont Graduate University showed, there is actually a chemical underpinning to this. That warm and fuzzy feeling you get when you help another person or give to someone else? That's the release of oxytocin in your body, which is the same hormone released during breast feeding or sex, and it has been linked to reducing blood pressure and cortisol levels.

Now, Elevate has two components: *serving others* and *serving the world*. Both of these concepts are rooted in ancient philosophy and religion as well as modern leadership research. Let's take a look at a few more of our Grand Philosophers to get a fuller picture of the parts of Elevate.

Grand Philosopher #1
Robert Greenleaf

Back in the early twentieth century, a young math major named Robert Greenleaf began working for AT&T, one of the largest corporations of the day. As he rose through the executive ranks of the telecommunications giant, Greenleaf developed a unique philosophy on the roles of leaders within organizations. For him, leaders were meant to serve both the needs of the organization *and* the employee (which ran counter to conventional management styles at the time). As Greenleaf put it, "The organization exists as much for the person as the person exists for the organization."

As his ideas on serving the needs of employees took hold during his tenure at AT&T, Greenleaf helped to promote the first females and the first African Americans to non-menial positions; the result was a more inclusive, productive workforce.

Then, after Greenleaf retired from AT&T, he sought to widen the reach of his ideas on servant-based leadership, extending beyond the context of corporate management to everyday living. In the 1970s, Greenleaf published several essays on the subject. In them, Greenleaf explored how societies (and not just businesses) can be impacted in a positive way when its members act selflessly and develop their purpose within the framework of serving others.

Coincidentally, the principles and practices that Greenleaf developed nearly half a century ago were partly inspired by the works and wisdom of Lao Tzu, one of our Grand Philosophers from the Reach element. Greenleaf recognized the ancient sage as an important voice that informed his ideas on Servant Leadership. As Lao Tzu remarked:

> The highest type of ruler is one of whose existence the people are barely aware . . . The Sage is self-effacing and scant of words. When his task is accomplished and things have been completed, all the people say, "We ourselves have achieved it!"

As you consider how Elevating others can be incorporated into your Vision, note that taking a serve-first mindset like the one Robert Greenleaf advocated leads to a more fulfilling life and engenders more caring around the world.

Grand Philosopher #2
Common Wisdom among Religious Traditions

The foundations and ideals of Elevate can often be described in more spiritual terms. That's because regardless of an individual's religious beliefs, many of our modern conceptions of what it means to live a "good and purposeful life"—even as seen through a secular lens—have been derived from religious principles.

There is common wisdom among many religious traditions. Many religions promote a sense of community and concern for your neighbour. They encourage hope and healing, help for those in need, and a "lifting up" of our needs, our challenges, and each other.

Hebrew scriptures encourage generosity not just in money and time but also in service and action, through love and kindness to others. In fact, within the eighteen morning blessings that are said each day are the charitable words and ideas of "clothing the naked" and "raising the downtrodden." As part of the preparation for their bar/ bat mitzvahs, many young Jewish men and women are also encouraged to take on a service project, or mitzvah project, to address some community need.

One of the pillars of the Islamic faith is about charity. Teachings in the Quran recommend charity and care for those in need in the form of both kindness and donations: "Help one another in acts of piety and righteousness."

At the same time, the Christian tradition holds Christ as an example of the "servant leader," one who would wash the feet of his own disciples. Indeed, many of the stories from the Bible were meant to inspire concern for your neighbour and charity for those in need. One of those stories, often referred to as "the loaves and the fishes," in which Jesus fed thousands of people with limited food supplies, is the same name that is often given to church soup kitchens around the world that serve the homeless and hungry. Additionally, the many Jesuit educational institutions that are part of the Catholic Church call upon their students to be "men and women for others."

Notions of generosity and philanthropy are also threaded through Buddhism, Sikhism, and Mormonism as well as many other world religions.

The takeaway here should be that although many of these religions might not agree on all of their principles and practices, it seems significant that they all emphasize, if not mandate, the need to give of yourself to your community, to lift up those around you. In the No Barriers life, we want you to consider your own obligation of giving to others and your wider role within your community, both locally and globally. Whether you are religious or not, start asking yourself how you can frame your Vision in a way that benefits others.

ELEVATE IN PRACTICE
Fred Rogers

Yes, as in *Mister Rogers*. The man who donned a sweater and sneakers each day as he invited young children and their imaginations into the Neighborhood of Make Believe. Fred Rogers spent his life manifesting the element of Elevate, using the medium of television as a platform to help children navigate the spectrum of complicated human emotions and teach them how to resolve everyday conflicts.

Years before he began *Mister Rogers' Neighborhood*, Fred Rogers knew that he wanted to find a way to help kids deal with the adversities that childhood can present. When Rogers was a young child himself, he struggled with shyness. In his words, he was a chubby boy who was picked on by other kids in his neighbourhood. This left Rogers feeling lonely, and he often depended on imaginary play, using his stuffed animals and puppets to create worlds and scenarios. As Rogers grew older, he learned how to overcome emotional obstacles, and he became determined to equip children with the tools they need to help others, providing those same tools that got him through the more challenging moments of childhood.

In his twenties, Fred Rogers joined the seminary and became an ordained minister, intent on ministering to children. Rogers's vision was always linked to childhood development, but he quickly learned that traditional ministering would be less effective in the era of moving images and airwaves. He realized that the easiest way to reach his sought-after audience was through the television. As Rogers studied the medium, he concluded that the offerings for children on television in the early 1960s were not conducive to cultivating young minds. In fact, the cartoon violence and frenetic pacing were detrimental to childhood development.

Rogers decided he would counterprogram the noisy, chaotic kids' television series with a gentler, quieter, and more musical format that would prompt the children to engage their imaginations and explore their emotions, rather than be passive observers. Each episode, the mild-mannered, silver-haired Mister Rogers would guide his young viewers through songs and scenarios that would reassure children that their feelings and thoughts were manageable. Often, Mister Rogers would find ways to put even the most challenging subjects into a language that children could understand—from racial discrimination, to divorce, to political violence, to death. While programs like *Sesame Street* were focusing on reading and math skills to prepare children for academics, *Mister Rogers' Neighborhood* was promoting emotional literacy in hopes of readying them for the social, moral, and ethical challenges of life.

And with Fred Rogers's new brand of educational entertainment came a simple yet impactful message on community:

> All of us, at some time or other, need help. Whether we're giving or receiving help, each of us has something valuable to bring to this world. That's one of the things that connects us as neighbours—in our own way, each one of us is a giver and a receiver.

Sound familiar? Although Fred Rogers may not have used the word "Elevate," he certainly applied the tenets of the Life Element. One of his most common themes was community, and his core goal was finding ways to better the world. For Fred Rogers, this goal extended beyond his time taping his children's show at the studio. In fact, he structured his entire day around the concept of lifting up others. He spent his mornings praying for those who had asked him for prayers, and he spent his evenings reading and responding to letters from viewers, even sending personalized birthday cards to many of them. He kept this schedule day in and day out over the course of more than three decades as his program reached millions of children.

By all accounts, Fred Rogers was the same off camera as he was on camera, his selflessness always evident. In fact, there's a very telling moment that took place during the 1997 Emmy Awards show. During the telecast, Fred Rogers was being honoured with a Lifetime Achievement Award. Although he takes a brief moment to thank those people who helped get him to that stage, Rogers quickly turns the spotlight back on the audience filled with celebrities, saying, "All of us have special ones who have loved us into being. Would you just take—along with me— ten seconds to think of the people who have helped you become who you are. Ten seconds of silence. I'll watch the time." The roomful of celebrities complied. During those ten seconds, the camera captured the faces of people who were surprised by their own tears and deep emotions.

Just imagine, Fred Rogers took a moment meant to be about him, and he made it about everyone else, lifting them up through ten seconds of reflection on their own successes and journeys. That's Elevate.

Pat Lafferty

With Fred Rogers being a classic example of *serving the world*, Pat Lafferty's story is one of *serving others* in a leadership role (not unlike the principles of servant leadership that Robert Greenleaf outlined).

After growing up in Upstate New York, Pat Lafferty attended a small liberal arts college on an ROTC scholarship. His experience in ROTC led him to be commissioned as a second lieutenant after undergrad, and he was stationed in Germany before being deployed to the desert in the Iraq-Kuwait War. It was during his seven years as an army officer that Pat first discovered the "we" (vs. "me") approach to life; he would carry this approach with him in every endeavour that followed.

After having spent seven years serving in the army as a platoon leader and company commander, Patrick made the decision to transition to the next phase of his journey, a return to civilian life. He was confronted with forging a new, yet-to-be-determined career. In deciding what path to pursue, he took stock of his own experiences and skillsets and evaluated a wide range of different career options.

After a thorough exploration, Pat took a job with a world-renowned advertising agency, Leo Burnett. Although some looked at Pat's transition from the army to advertising as odd, Pat understood that there were many similarities between the two worlds and that his experiences in the military had, in fact, uniquely prepared him for this industry change, because the army for him was a study in human nature.

As Pat says, "So much of what I did in the army was about understanding people, whether it was the people I was leading or the people in the countries where I was working." Oftentimes in the army, he had to lead people in challenging circumstances, providing them with the support and motivation to do things that were outside their comfort zones but necessary for his platoon to fulfil its mission.

Early in his advertising career, Pat stood out from his peers because of his knack for creating strong teams in which each person was both valued for his or her unique skills and motivated to overperform to help the team succeed. As he rose up the ranks of the agency world, he had the rare opportunity to serve the army as a client. His world had now come full circle. His army training, which had prepared him for his advertising training, was now benefiting from both his current and former vocations. Under Pat's leadership, his agency team managed all of the army's public-facing communications including advertising, PR, and digital marketing—with such deep insight and understanding of the army that no other agency could offer.

Over the next few decades, Pat continued to be promoted in the agency world and with Discovery Communications, as he worked on global brand platforms for Fortune 500 companies. Even though he took satisfaction from each new successful advertising campaign and series he launched, he felt there was something missing from his job.

For Pat, there was a genuine sense of achievement when he could help others reach their full potential, and he developed an unrelenting desire to help and lift up others. It was only when he finally secured an opportunity to lead an agency that Pat began to feel truly fulfilled in his career.

He adopted a Servant Leadership approach, and this set him and his employees up for success. As he says, "It's important to be a leader that serves others, because people respond and achieve when others believe in them. They rise to the occasion and do more than they can."

With his passion for elevating others, it is no wonder that he crossed paths with us at No Barriers. In fact, Pat Lafferty has been an ongoing advisor to our organization, including helping us define the Life Elements within the context of corporate leadership. Patrick is wired to Elevate people like no one else we've seen in our community, and we often cite his relentless desire to lift up others— whether in his unit back in the army, his team at the ad agency, or other members of his community.

HOW TO ELEVATE

Does this mean we're going to ask you to go back to your Vision and make sure it is about much more than just you? Well, yes. Let's get started.

Step 1. Complete your Roadmap.

Return to your Roadmap where you wrote "You Are Here" at the top of the page, your Vision at the bottom, and a series of Reach goals in the space between. Consider the work you've done in this book related to Pioneer, Rope Team, Alchemy, and Summits, and add any relevant visual cues or words to your Roadmap that feel important to represent. Like any good map, you want this to point you in the right direction and remind you of the elements you found to be most important on your journey so far.

Now pause and take a look at your map. What emotions does it evoke? For many, it will instil a sense of excitement and anticipation mixed with trepidation. How much is your journey about you versus others? How much is about the world outside of you versus the world inside of you?

Step 2. Adapt your Vision to incorporate the principle of Elevate.

With the principle of Elevate in mind and your Roadmap sitting right in front of you, think: "How might this be about others more than it's about me? Where might I Elevate my team, my family, my community, or the world around me as part of my journey?"

Here's an example to spark your ideas. Let's bring you all the way back to chapter 1 where we introduced you to Erik Weihenmayer and recall his Vision Statement:

> To find a way to lead despite my own fears, to push myself beyond my understanding of what I'm capable of, and to always be a good partner and friend.

You can see how part of his Vision is definitely introspective and self-driven. But the second part of his

Vision is all about others—being a good "partner and friend."

Now rewrite your personal Vision in light of this new reflection.

Step 3. Share your revised Vision with a close friend or family member.

It's time to take your Vision and share it with someone close to you. Why? For two reasons. First, the simple act of confiding in someone else will make all of your work from this book begin to move out of your head and into reality. Second, someone else needs to tell you whether your Vision has elements of *me* and *we* in it. Oftentimes, we're so locked in our own worlds that we forget that outside perspective will broaden our possibilities. In your discussion with your confidant, explain a bit about your journey and your Roadmap. Here are a few suggested things to discuss:

- My Vision is meant to be about more than just me. It should help me Elevate others or the world around me. When you hear my Vision as I've written it, do you get this sense of both the *me* and the *we*?
- What questions come to your mind when I read you my Vision Statement?
- What ideas does my Vision Statement spark for you?

After your discussion, make any final changes to your Vision Statement and your Roadmap. You're just about ready to move on to the final chapter and take your No Barriers Pledge!

Before we do that, let's go back to Whitney and learn how she chose to Elevate and how profound her Vision became as a result.

LIVING WITHOUT SHAME

When Whitney had clicked on her mousepad to post the video of her dancing to Jason Derulo's "Talk Dirty," she had no idea what to expect. The truth was, Whitney didn't feel like she was doing this for herself. She was fine with her body now—in fact, she loved it. She wanted to post the video more for others. Without knowing it, she wanted to Elevate the community of people who, for too long, had suffered from their own body shame. Her highest hope was that other people would see her dancing, find it liberating, and in turn, attempt to overcome their own insecurities. But the reaction to her video on YouTube far exceeded her expectations.

During that first week after she posted the video in her series "A Fat Girl Dances," the number of views just kept ticking up as thousands of people—and then hundreds of thousands of people—watched her shake and wiggle and kick across the dance floor. They made comments like "Omg. You're amazing. Such an inspiration," and "I have spent my whole life being ashamed of my body. What a sad waste of time," and "I wish I had the confidence to dance in public!"

As another week went by, Whitney watched in disbelief as more than a million people clicked on her video. It was unimaginable to Whitney that all these people would be tuning in to watch her dance; and, in that moment, she had the sense that the earth was moving beneath her feet. Her life was changing.

And that's when the phone started ringing.

The first call was from *Huffington Post*, who wanted to write a piece about her and the body positivity movement. Then it was a producer from *Inside Edition* who wanted to interview her on television. Then someone from *The Steve Harvey Show*. Then *Good Morning America*. Then the *Today* show. The calls just kept coming. The world wanted to hear Whitney Way Thore's story.

As it turned out, *Today* would be Whitney's first televised interview. Not even a month after she first posted the video, she travelled with her family to New York City to be on the morning program. Whitney sat for the interview with Hoda Kotb and Kathie Lee Gifford, with her parents and her brother sitting in the audience. As she discussed her lifelong struggle with her weight and promoted self-acceptance, Whitney caught a glimpse of her father out of the corner of her eye: he was quietly crying.

After the show, Whitney privately asked her father why he was upset. He told her that as he watched her speak so passionately about body image issues, he was impressed with his daughter. Her father then hugged her, and as more tears came, he said, "I know I told you that you couldn't change the world, but I think you already are."

Not long after her string of talk show interviews and magazine features, Whitney received a call from the TLC network. One of the execs invited her to fly out to LA to discuss a possible reality series—starring Whitney. After hopping on a plane and hearing the pitch from the network execs, Whitney realized how the show could benefit not just herself but also other people like her. She believed deeply that the easiest way she could Elevate other people was to let them see her living her life authentically (and imperfectly). The network shot a pilot episode for *My Big Fat Fabulous Life* with Whitney and her family and friends, then greenlit the show for a series. Before Whitney knew it, she was a reality star, a reality star with a message: *Live the life you want right now.*

In the five years since she began her life anew, Whitney has continued to seek out ways to Elevate other people. She has become a powerful voice in the body positive movement, and she began the #NoBodyShame campaign, which advocates for living a life of passion through what she calls "radical self-love." Whitney is now in the seventh season of *My Big Fat Fabulous Life* (and she just got engaged). For Whitney, she believes that once you have overcome some adversity in your life, it becomes about lifting up other people.

Conclusion

Beyond Barriers

*"You may encounter many defeats,
but you must not be defeated. In fact, it may be
necessary to encounter the defeats, so you can
know who you are, what you can rise from,
how you can still come out of it."*
—*Maya Angelou*

Patient ID #6048680 laid silently in his dark hospital room in New York City listening to a group of medical experts outside his doors discuss his life-threatening prognosis. He knew these doctors. They were his friends. Only weeks ago, he had been working alongside them to treat patients in this very same hospital.

Dr. Andres Maldonado was twenty-seven years old and had been in perfectly good health up until nine days ago, when he had a case of the chills. Fever and chest tightness followed closely thereafter. He tested positive for COVID-19, but being young and healthy (and a doctor himself), he felt he could weather this storm. Andres monitored himself closely as his condition deteriorated. After nine days, his brother, also a doctor, finally ordered him to take action: "Get your butt to the ER." With that brotherly shove, Andres made his first visit to Jacobi Medical Center as a patient.

He was in his third year of residency at the hospital in the Bronx, New York. Andres's story of success is a by-product of his family's emphasis on hard work and education. As a young man, Andres's father escaped as a refugee from the civil war in El Salvador to come to America, and his first job was as a dishwasher in New York City. Over time, he married and had children. Andres, inspired by the stories of his accomplished and hardworking father, was stoic and proud like his father, giving his all to his studies and offering zero complaints. When Andres became a doctor, he not only felt satisfied for himself, but he had also validated his parents' many sacrifices.

Now, no longer able to treat himself, he was admitted to the hospital—an acknowledgment that no matter how strong he was, he needed help. Later that evening, alone in his room, the tears came rushing out. It was the first time he had cried in a long time. He had been bottling up all of his feelings and his fears. All of the worry that he might be seriously ill, the stress of having tried and failed to heal himself, and the need to stay strong in front of his parents all came rushing out at once. It was a moment of clarity in which he finally shed his emotional mask and the baggage that he was carrying. He was able to see himself for who he was at that moment: not the stoic, successful, tireless ER doc, but the vulnerable COVID-19 patient who was scared for his life. And with that release of tears and embrace of his struggle, he was able to clearly focus on the fight for his recovery.

Andres was taken to the ICU and placed on a high-flow nasal cannula to force oxygen into his lungs. At first, it didn't have much of an effect, and he worried that his doctors would need to intubate him, but they kept trying. His Rope Team was there to support him through it all. His brother, his girlfriend, and his parents would talk to him on the phone. Every day, his many friends from the hospital would come up to his room lifting his spirit. After a while, Andres was breathing a bit better. After six days, his lungs had cleared and he was discharged. But he will never be the same.

Andres's discharge papers sit on top of his bedroom dresser as an everyday reminder of his experience as a patient. He took a few weeks off to regain his strength; in that time, he reflected on how this ordeal had affected his life. The reason Andres originally went into medicine was to help people who were sick. Through this experience, he learned that a big part of helping people is understanding and addressing what it is that they are feeling. This includes making himself fully present to listen to patients who are visibly scared and understanding that some patients could be hiding very real fears but not communicating them (like he was). He also now has a greater sensitivity for patients who are feeling shame and embarrassment around needing help with basic human needs. As a patient, Andres could not walk to the bathroom and was horrified of the thought of having a nurse wipe him, so he held it in. He returned to work at the hospital with newfound focus on bringing greater empathy to each of his patients, giving attention to their needs, and speaking openly about his personal experience as a patient.

YOU HAVE THE TOOLS

Now, more than ever, the world needs to believe that what's within us is stronger than what's in our way. Like Andres, we are all one step away from the unexpected. Even though life has been this way since the beginning of time, it feels more poignant and real than ever before. Throughout this book, in fact, we've introduced you to many people, including ourselves, whose life was cruising along before something drastically, and often unexpectedly, interrupted it. Life is indeed full of many barriers.

It has been said that adversity introduces a person to him- or herself; but let us add this: it's only once a person harnesses that adversity that he or she knows what he or she is truly capable of. Over the course of this book, our objective has been to take you through a process of self-discovery to help you work through a current barrier in your life, with the hope that you will carry forward this new knowledge and use it to work through future barriers.

By introducing you to the Life Elements, we have equipped you with strategies that break down your obstacle into manageable parts, and we have guided you through the internal considerations and emotional exercises that will help you overcome the specific challenges you face.

Along the way, we have asked a lot of you.

For starters, we have asked you to be completely honest with yourself, which is no small feat. As you have no doubt observed, the high level of self-examination required by the Life Elements forces you to take a deep and penetrating look at the choices you make and the attitudes you adopt. We have all created ways to hide or ignore our unhealthier habits and behaviours as well as our ingrained negativity; and finally admitting to these aspects of ourselves—which is crucial to harnessing all of one's strengths—can be taxing emotionally and physically.

We have also pressed you to confront some of the toughest questions this life offers you—beginning with no less than your *Why*. We know how tempting it is to turn away from these questions rather than do the hard work of searching for answers. Just admitting you don't have all the answers already is a genuine act of humility, and it's the reason we spend most of our time as humans distracting ourselves by swiping through our Facebook feeds or binge-watching a Netflix series. Considering the *Why* of your life can be a difficult and discomfiting task; but at No Barriers, we know that facing this question is the only effective method for pushing through adversity in a lasting way.

And, of course, once you were able to pinpoint your *Why*, we asked you to engage in a series of challenging exercises that can deliver you a better sense of the *How*. For us, it's not enough just to discover your compass; you need the map as well. Each activity within the Life Elements is designed to help delineate that map to your specific obstacle.

All that is to say that you have done some heavy lifting to get to this moment, and we're excited that you have journeyed with us this far. The reason we have been working in this field for the past few decades—and the original motivation for us to begin the No Barriers organization—is our desire to give people the tools they need to overcome any adversity. Our sincere and profound hope for you is that the process has helped you get beyond the barrier that brought you to this book in the first place.

THE NO BARRIERS LIFE

One thing we know is, even once you have overcome a particular adversity in your life, there will always be more obstacles ahead of you. From where you're standing right now, maybe you can't see around the corner to know what's coming—a career change, a challenging relationship, an illness—but you can be prepared for it. That is why we have designed No Barriers not as a one-time solution but as a way of life.

As you have engaged in the activities and personal explorations assigned in each of the Life Elements, you have been developing the habits and the mindset necessary for taking on future adversities. In addition, you have learned how to live in alignment with your values, and this has created a solid foundation for you to build on.

Now that you have read through the book once and built out your toolkit, you have a resource you can return to over and over again as new challenges arise. In the same way an athlete has to practice each day in order to stay at the top of their game, you'll want to revisit the sections of the book you find most helpful to you.

So, as you reach the final pages of this book, let's do a quick refresher on the Life Elements in an effort to fortify your No Barriers Life.

VISION. Your Vision is about the core values that animate you and how you can harness those values to reveal a foundational and sustainable purpose in your life. In Aristotle's estimation, your Vision is "activity of the soul in accordance with virtue."

One of the key takeaways in this Life Element is the distinction between a goal and a Vision: a goal allows you to reach a certain point in your life, whereas a Vision gives your life a point. Remember, when you are crafting your Vision Statement, it's about much more than naming a list of goals or desired achievements. It's a qualitative endeavour, not a quantitative one; your Vision Statement should be focused on your values and beliefs that can be a guiding light.

Since the concept of purpose is also crucial to Vision, another lesson to keep in mind going forward is that purpose is a better compass than happiness. Remember the reason Viktor Frankl gives for this? Your life is filled with unexpected events that will suddenly strip you of that desired feeling of happiness; if happiness is the one thing you want from life, what do you do in such moments? How do you endure times of suffering? Do not confuse the short-term emotion of happiness with the long-term human need for meaning. Remember, happiness follows meaning, not the other way around.

Finally, Vision is not an unchanging thing, and you must allow yourself to fail. Although you may want to "just know" what you're supposed to do with your life, for your purpose to be spelled out for you, that's not how a calling works. And that's exactly what Vision is—it's a *calling*.

REACH. This is where you embrace any adversity that is present in your life right now and choose to use it as a way to grow. Think about what action you are going to take to move closer to the purpose you have adopted for yourself. You are not tackling the adversity all at once; you are breaking it down into manageable pieces and finding a good place to start.

At the centre of Reach is your ability to step outside of your comfort zone. In doing so, you will discover opportunities to grow that were not immediately apparent to you, you will increase your self-confidence, and you will build deeper relationships with people around you as you allow yourself to trust others.

And remember the wisdom we borrowed from Lao Tzu: You don't need to stress about the entire journey that lies ahead of you; instead, all you need to do to Reach is take the first step. It is often the hardest step, but once it is taken, those that follow become easier. Also, sometimes it's a process of trial and error, which implies that you may fail; and when you do, it's important to not let those moments keep you from moving forward.

ALCHEMY. This element is all about developing the right mindset. It's about cultivating a spirit of optimism and positivity despite the adversities that you must confront. When you become an Alchemist, you realize that your old way of thinking about something no longer fits. You've broken your own mould and crafted a new worldview. It's a view that believes in every adversity lies a tremendous opportunity.

Your ability to reframe your own mindset is linked to your understanding of choice. Remember the story of Epictetus, the enslaved cripple who was ultimately freed? His journey taught you that once you can determine where in your life you have the ability to choose and where you do not, you will find it easier to frame your own mindset. As Epictetus said, "To make the best of what is in our power, and take the rest as it occurs."

Another key component to Alchemy is deactivating the negativity in your life. It's easy to dwell on the negative aspects and fall into a cycle of rumination. You can stop these cycles by redirecting your attention to another activity—even doing something as simple as going for a walk. Just make sure you give your full attention to that other activity. By clearing away the negativity, you are allowing optimism and hope to move into that abandoned space—and those are the things that can be fuel for breaking through your adversity.

PIONEERING. These are your guiding words in this element: *have a fearless belief in a future that does not yet exist.* Here, you are developing systems and tools that will help you find creative ways to work through your most difficult challenges.

To succeed, invariably you will have to fail first, often many times. Accept this reality, and then have the freedom to experiment with solutions. Do not seek perfection because you know it rarely exists. Introduce new ways of looking at problems. These are mindsets that an inventor uses; you will need to become an inventor to create your needed solutions. Also, internalize the lessons of design thinking: have the confidence to know that there are solutions out there to your problem, even if you don't find them on your first attempt.

Here are the other key activities that will assist you in Pioneering: get outside your own head and consult others who have experience with your particular problem; brainstorm solutions that bring you closer to achieving your Reach (there are no bad ideas); scale down your list of possible solutions and begin experimenting; assess what you have learned and then pivot if necessary. Ultimately, remember that Pioneering is an iterative process and you will learn by doing.

ROPE TEAM. Having a support system is critical to overcoming most adversities. This element is about having the right friends to support you emotionally and finding those people who can support you intellectually and physically as well. Building the right Rope Team will help ensure you have the best chance at carrying out your Vision.

We are in an age where the true meaning of friendship has been diluted and even confused by social media, where relationships require little more effort than the click of a "like" button. Having an On-Rope friend means having someone in your life who will be at your side through thick and thin, someone who will provide counsel, and someone who promotes your physical and mental health. As Aristotle points out, a true friendship is a two-way street: they give their all for you, and you for them. Such a friendship moves both parties forward through adversity and in the direction of each other's purpose.

In choosing your Rope Team, you will need to assess your current relationships and decide what might be missing within your support system. (You will also weed out any toxic relationships that might be adding unwanted negativity.) While you should not see your On-Rope relationships as strictly transactional, you do want to ensure that you have the right type of support that this situation demands. This might mean reaching outside of your current network and finding those people well-versed in your particular adversity.

Last, your Rope Team can have an outsized effect on your mood and mindset, which can have an impact on your success. Put simply, your tribe determines your vibe.

SUMMITS. Pause and appreciate how far you've come. It's often difficult to stop and reflect on your journey when you are right in the middle of it. But in these moments of looking back, you will recognize Summits that you didn't realize you had passed along the way.

The first crucial element to Summits is reflection. Throughout your day, your attention is being pulled in a thousand and one directions—from work emails to social media feeds. In order to create the space for reflection, you will need to train your attention through techniques such as meditation and scheduling daily check-ins with your mind.

Gratitude, the other key component of Summits, is the act of appreciating those people and relationships and achievements already in your life. Although you rarely think about the rewards of gratitude, it has noticeable and positive impacts on your mental and physical health. It also gives you energy for the remainder of your journey ahead.

ELEVATE. Now take what you've learned on this journey and share it with others. The human experience is universal, which means the things you're enduring are likely the same things others need help with, too.

The principles of this element are rooted in the notion that when we make our Vision about much more than ourselves, not only do we receive much more fulfilment for ourselves, but we also unleash great power in others. When you start to look outside yourself and your own growth and think about how you can lift up others around you, you create a cascading effect that will lead to stronger, healthier communities.

One of the nice side effects of the Elevate element is that when you help others, it actually benefits your own health and well-being. Recent science shows that giving to others around you can actually be a boon to your health, both physically and mentally, giving your system a jolt of oxytocin.

Ultimately, when you widen your Vision to include the welfare of others, and when you become a part of someone else's support system, you open yourself up to the best parts of life. Remember, true happiness is found in helping others.

THE FRIENDS WE'VE MADE ALONG THE ROAD

We've already told you about our lifelong friendship with each other, a bond that allowed us to help found No Barriers together. Now it's time to pull back the curtain on some of the other friendships that have been foundational to the No Barriers movement.

In each chapter, we have profiled one person that we believe exemplifies that particular Life Element; but the truth is, we didn't have to look far for those exemplars because each of those people—Erik, Mandy, J.R., Hugh, Gretchen, Kyle, and Whitney—are already in the No Barriers community and have become dear friends of ours.

Each year, many of them participate in our annual event, the No Barriers Summit, as participants, activity leaders, or speakers. For many of our attendees and even a few of our exemplars, the No Barriers Summit served as that necessary spark that has defined their Vision and kickstarted their journey. Before Mandy Harvey earned the AGT Golden Buzzer singing "Try," she was performing it at one of our events. Before Kyle Maynard was the subject of the ESPN documentary about his climb up Mount Kilimanjaro, he was learning how he could bear-claw his way to the top of a mountain with No Barriers.

Perhaps the greatest aspect about the No Barriers Summit is that it brings together an entire community of people who are both pushing themselves and each other through their respective struggles. We invite you to join a No Barriers experience—whether it's an online course, a podcast, or an in-person experience, such as our No Barriers Summit. The next great No Barriers story is waiting to be written, and we want it to be your story, written by you.

THE NO BARRIERS FLAG

We've spent seven chapters walking you through the No Barriers Life Elements, and even though we are approaching the end of our storytelling, it's far from the end of your No Barriers story. In fact, we hope that it is just the beginning.

If you visit the No Barriers website (NoBarriersUSA. org) or any of our social media pages, it won't take you long before you see the iconic **No Barriers Flag**. It is our signature symbol that you will see in almost every No Barriers event and photograph. It is an almost square white flag, nearly one foot by one foot, with two small grommets at the top. The message in the middle is very simple: "No Barriers" beneath our logo. Along with the flag is a warning label that reads:

WARNING: DO NOT HANDLE WITH CARE. This is not a fragile item. It is as strong as your will and determination. For anyone seeking to accomplish goals that others may have thought were impossible, outrageous, audacious, ridiculous, worthless, a flat-out-waste-of-time, and/or silly, bring this along for your journey. When you arrive at YOUR summit, fly your flag, relish your triumph, and have someone snap a picture.

Over the past several years, people from around the country and the globe have sent their pictures to us. The photos show people sharing their triumph at the end of their struggle: the wounded veteran standing on a mountaintop, the girl receiving her college diploma, the cancer patient completing his treatment, and the runner making it across her finish line. The list goes on and on.

But what we find most interesting in hearing stories from thousands of people who have received our flag is that while they send in the photo at the end of the journey, its most important role is in the middle of the struggle.

That's where the flag serves the critical role as a day-to-day reminder of a bigger goal. We know that all over the world, people are hanging their flags where they need them most—on the wall of the rehabilitation centre or behind the desk or on the mirror—as a daily reminder of their Reach goals and their Vision. We hope the next flag that we send out is to you.

NO BARRIERS PLEDGE

This is it. Your final assignment: Write and Submit Your No Barriers Pledge. Pledges are a part of No Barriers traditions. A pledge is your commitment to your continued progress toward your Vision.

Pull out your Roadmap again and identify one of your Reach goals that you can achieve in the next fifteen to thirty days. If you're striving for a habitual practice, choose something you can make into a daily or weekly routine in that period. Here are some examples that we've seen from others:

- "Finding an expert, or Sherpa, to talk to me about how I can best carry out my Vision"
- "Prioritizing health as a part of my daily routine"
- "Taking a few hours a week to care for an important relationship that I've neglected"

Although your Pledge should be one of your Reach goals, we remind you that it is a declaration of your commitment to your ongoing personal growth and how you will Elevate others. Also, by taking this pledge, you become part of our tribe.

1. Visit NoBarriersUSA.org/WhatsWithinYou.
2. Type in your No Barriers Pledge. (It's okay if you changed or added new language or ideas to it from your original Roadmap.)
3. Submit, and we'll send you a virtual No Barriers Flag.

We care about your progress toward your Vision and hope we can help you get there. Submitting your Pledge was a big step.

So, as we say goodbye for now, we leave you with our motto, one that has helped so many in our No Barriers community as they have worked to overcome their own adversities:

What's Within You Is Stronger
Than What's In Your Way.

Bibliography

These are the books, articles, websites, and videos that are either referenced in this book or from which we drew direct inspiration. Every one of these is worth checking out!

INTRODUCTION

Frankl, Viktor. *Man's Search for Meaning.* Boston, MA: Beacon, 1946.

Wilson, E.O. *Consilience: The Unity of Knowledge.* New York, NY: Vintage Books, 1999.

VISION

Aristotle. *Nicomachean Ethics.* The Internet Classics Archive.

Brooks, David. "Should You Live for Your Résumé or Your Eulogy?" Filmed March 2014, at TED2014. Video, 4:49, https://www.ted.com/talks/david_brooks_should_you_live_for_your_resume_or_your_eulogy?language=en.

Frankl, Viktor. *Man's Search for Meaning*. Boston, MA: Beacon, 1946.

Frankl, Viktor. "Youth in Search of Meaning." Filmed 1972, in Toronto, Canada. Video, 4:21, https://logotherapy.univie.ac.at/assets/vid/clip_toronto_72.mp4.

Kaufman, Scott. "The Differences between Happiness and Meaning in Life." *Scientific American*, January 30, 2016, https://blogs.scientificamerican.com/beautiful-minds/the-differences-between-happiness-and-meaning-in-life/.

Stoltz, Paul, and Weihenmayer, Erik. *The Adversity Advantage*. New York: A Fireside Book, 2006.

Weihenmayer, Erik. Interview by Larry King. *Larry King Live*, CNN, June 6, 2012. Video, https://www.youtube.com/watch?v=tGM4y3ajXO0.

Weihenmayer, Erik. Interview by Oprah Winfrey. *Oprah*, August 31, 2012. Video, https://www.youtube.com/watch?v=GKlGXHzbyPY.

Weihenmayer, Erik. *Touch the Top of the World: A Blind Man's Journey to Climb Farther than the Eye Can See*. New York, NY: Dutton Adult, 2001.

Winfrey, Oprah. "Every Person Has a Purpose." Oprah.com, , https://www.oprah.com/spirit/how-oprah-winfrey-found-her-purpose.

REACH

America's Got Talent. Episode 1202. NBC, June 2017, https://www.youtube.com/watch?v=oHUuCLgfMpo.

Duhigg, Charles. *The Power of Habit: Why We Do What We Do in Life and Business.* New York: Random House, 2012.

Harvey, Mandy. "Mandy Harvey: A Not Impossible Help One, Help Many Story." Filmed 2019 by Not Impossible Labs. Video, 9:38.

Harvey, Mandy. *Sensing the Rhythm: Finding My Voice in a World without Sound.* New York, NY: Howard Books, 2017.

Molinsky, Andy. *Reach: A New Strategy to Help You Step outside Your Comfort Zone, Rise to the Challenge, and Build Confidence.* New York, NY: Avery, 2017.

PIONEER

Baehr, Leslie. "Hugh Herr Is a Leading Bionic Researcher— But the Story that Got Him There Is Tragic." *Business Insider,* August 14, 2014, https://www.businessinsider.com.au/bionics-researcher-hugh-herrs-mountaineering-accident-2014-8.

Balf, Todd. "The Biomechatronic Man." Outside, September 6, 2017, https://www.outsideonline.com/2238401/biomechatronic-man.

Brown, Tim, "Designers—Think Big!" Filmed July 2009, at TEDGlobal 2009 Video, 16:35, https://www.ted.com/talks/tim_brown_designers_think_big?utm_campaign=tedspread&utm_medium=referral&utm_source=tedcomshare.

Dweck, Carol. "The Power of Believing That You Can Improve." Filmed November 2014, at TEDxNorrkoping.

Video, 10:13, https://www.ted.com/talks/carol_dweck_the_power_of_believing_that_you_can_improve?utm_campaign=tedspread&utm_medium=referral&utm_source=tedcomshare.

Herr, Hugh. "How We'll Become Cyborgs and Extend Human Potential." Filmed April 2018, at TED2018. Video, 15:16, https://www.ted.com/talks/hugh_herr_how_we_ll_become_cyborgs_and_extend_human_potential?language=en.

IDEO. "History of Design Thinking," https://designthinking.ideo.com/history.

Mindset Works, https://www.mindsetworks.com.

Osius, Alison. *Second Ascent: The Story of Hugh Herr.* Mechanicsburg, PA: Stackpole Books, 1991.

Rowling, J. K. Harvard University Commencement Speech, Cambridge, MA, June 5, 2008. Video, 20:58, https://www.youtube.com/watch?v=wHGqp8lz36c&feature=youtu.be.

Stanford d.school, https://dschool.stanford.edu/.

ALCHEMY

60 Minutes. "The Long Road Home from Iraq," segment including J. R. Martinez. CBS, December 1, 2003, https://www.cbsnews.com/news/the-long-road-home-from-iraq/.

Achor, Shawn. *The Happiness Advantage: The Seven Principles of Positive Psychology That Fuel Success and Performance at Work.* New York, NY: Currency, 2010.

CBS Evening News. "J. R. Martinez's Story of Survival." CBS, November 23, 2011, https://www.youtube.com/watch?v=DrZsQMQ_Q7s.

Fredrickson, Barbara. *Positivity.* New York, NY: Harmony, 2009.

Heuser, Stephen. "Good as Gold: What Alchemists Got Right." *The Boston Globe*, March 15, 2009, http://archive.boston.com/bostonglobe/ideas/articles/2009/03/15/good_as_gold/?page=4.

Hochwald, Lambeth. "Robin Roberts on Surviving Two Life-Threatening Illnesses and What Healthy Looks Like." *Parade*, October 18, 2018, https://parade.com/707653/lhochwald/robin-roberts-on-surviving-two-life-threatening-illnesses-and-what-healthy-looks-like/.

Laozi. *Tao Te Ching.* New York, NY: Vintage Books, 1972.

Martinez, J. R. *Full of Heart: My Story of Survival, Strength and Spirit.* New York, NY: Hachette Books, 2012.

Seligman, Martin. *Learned Optimism.* New York: Knopf, 1991.

Seligman, Martin. "The New Era of Positive Psychology." Filmed February 2004, at TED2004, https://www.ted.com/talks/martin_seligman_the_new_era_of_positive_psychology?utm_campaign=tedspread&utm_medium=referral&utm_source=tedcomshare.

ROPE TEAM

Aristotle. *The Nicomachean Ethics.* Hertfordshire, Great Britain: Wordsworth Editions Limited, 1996.

Brown, Brené. "The Anatomy of Trust." Speech originally delivered at UCLA's Royce Hall, 2015. Video, 24:08, https://jamesclear.com/great-speeches/the-anatomy-of-trust-by-brene-brown.

Burton, Neel. "The Philosophy of Friendship." *Psychology Today*, September 6, 2017, https://www.psychologytoday.com/us/blog/hide-and-seek/201204/the-philosophy-friendship.

Collingwood, Jane. "The Importance of Friendship." *PsychCentral*, March 18, 2019, https://psychcentral.com/lib/the-importance-of-friendship/.

Duhigg, Charles. "What Google Learned from Its Quest to Build the Perfect Team." *The New York Times*, February 28, 2016, https://www.nytimes.com/2016/02/28/magazine/what-google-learned-from-its-quest-to-build-the-perfect-team.html?campaignId=7JFJX.

Evans, Gretchen. *Leading from the Front.* Scotts Valley, CA: CreateSpace, 2018.

Rath, Tom. *Vital Friends: The People You Can't Afford to Live Without.* New York, NY: Gallup Press, 2006.

Today. "*Today*'s New Puppy Has a Purpose: To Help Our Nation's Heroes." NBC, August 22, 2016, https://www.today.com/video/today-s-new-puppy-has-a-new-purpose-to-help-our-nation-s-heroes-748446787829.

Today. "Army Vet Tells Megyn Kelly How Her Service Dog Has Changed Her Life." NBC, April 18, 2018, https://www.msn.com/en-us/video/news/army-vet-tells-megyn-kelly-how-her-service-dog-has-changed-her-life/vp-AAw15lN.

SUMMITS

ESPN Profile. "Kyle Maynard." ESPN, March 4, 2012. Video, 11:20, https://www.youtube.com/watch?v=czXTkNyzF98.

Healthbeat. "Giving Thanks Can Make You Happier." Harvard Health Publishing, Harvard Medical School, https://www.health.harvard.edu/healthbeat/giving-thanks-can-make-you-happier.

Maynard, Kyle. *No Excuses: The True Story of a Congenital Amputee Who Became a Champion in Wrestling and in Life.* Washington, DC: Regnery, 2005.

Popova, Maria. "How We Think: John Dewey on the Art of Reflection and Fruitful Curiosity in an Age of Instant Opinions and Information Overload." BrainPickings, https://www.brainpickings.org/2014/08/18/how-we-think-john-dewey/.

Weihenmayer, Erik. "Let's Make Great Americans—Always." *The Denver Post,* April 3, 2017, https://www.denverpost.com/2017/04/03/lets-make-great-americans-always/.

ELEVATE

Ahmed, Kaitlin. "Fewer Americans Are Volunteering and Giving than at Any Time in the Last Two Decades." *Phys. org*, November 19, 2018, https://phys.org/news/2018-11-americans-volunteering-decades.html.

Junod, Tom. "Can You Say . . . Hero?" *Esquire*, November 1998, https://www.esquire.com/entertainment/tv/a27134/can-you-say-hero-esq1198/.

Rogers, Fred. Emmy Acceptance Speech, 24th Annual Daytime Emmy Awards, Los Angeles. March 26, 2008. Video, 3:12, https://www.youtube.com/watch?v=Upm9LnuCBUM.

Suttie, Jill, and Jason March. "5 Ways Giving Is Good for You." *Greater Good Magazine*, December 13, 2012, https://greatergood.berkeley.edu/article/item/5_ways_giving_is_good_for_you.

Tarallo, Mark. "The Art of Servant Leadership." SHRM, May 17, 2018, https://www.shrm.org/resourcesandtools/hr-topics/organizational-and-employee-development/pages/the-art-of-servant-leadership.aspx.

Thore, Whitney Way. *I Do It with the Lights On: And 10 More Discoveries on the Road to a Blissfully Shame-Free Life*. New York: Ballantine Books, 2016.

Thore, Whitney Way. "A Fat Girl Dancing." Original video filmed May 27, 2014. Video, 2:47.